The Macmillan Spectrum Investor's Choice Guide to

▼

Mutual Fund Investment Strategies

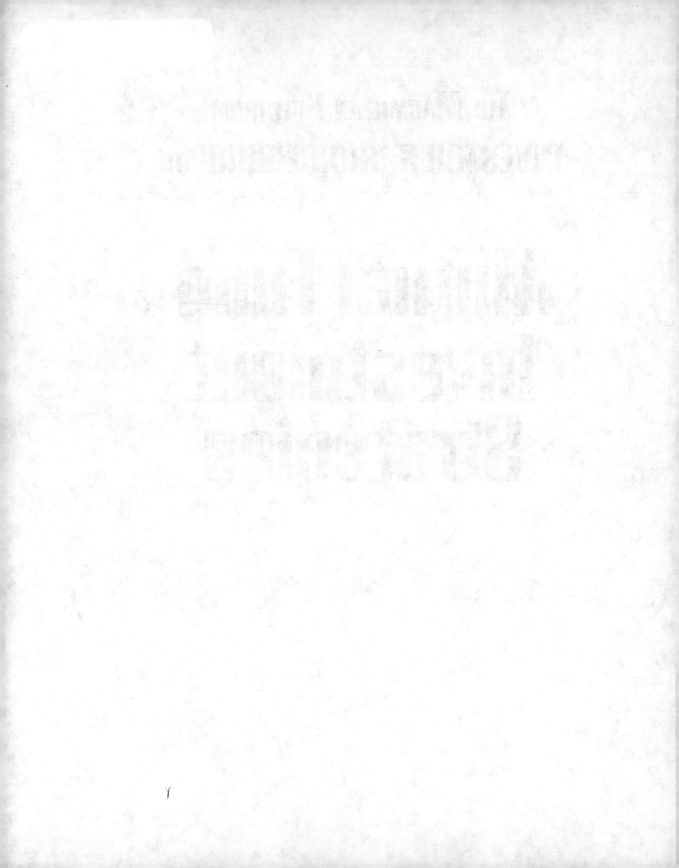

The Macmillan Spectrum

Investor's Choice Guide to

▼

Mutual Fund Investment Strategies

J.W. Dicks

Macmillan/Spectrum
New York

Macmillan/Spectrum

A Simon and Schuster Macmillan Company

1633 Broadway New York, NY 10019

Library of Congress Catalog Card Number: 97-071159

ISBN: 0-02861441-0

Manufactured in the United States of America

98 97 96   9 8 7 6 5 4 3 2 1

Book Design: A&D Howell

Cover Design: Kevin Hanek

To my mother, June Simmons Dicks, who taught me the rewards of setting a "little bit aside to invest for your future."

CONTENTS

▼

About the Author

▼

J.W. Dicks, a securities attorney and investment analyst, has been active in the invest-ment industry for 25 years. As a leading seminar instructor on financial topics, J.W. Dicks has traveled the country speaking to over 150,000 people on mutual funds, stocks, law, small business, and real estate. In addition to his lectures, he has written numerous articles, manuals, and newsletters on the same topics. Since 1989 he has published the *Mutual Fund Advisor,* a newsletter service for mutual fund investors. He is the author of *The American Dream, Financial C.P.R., The Florida Investor, The Small Business Legal Kit, The 100 Best Investments for Your Retirement, Mutual Fund Investing Strategies,* and *How to Incorporate and Operate Your Business.*

J.W. Dicks is the president and principal of Delta First Financial, Inc., a Registered Investment Advisor. Through his firm, Mr. Dicks was one of the first to offer Private Money Management services to small investors nationwide on a fee-only basis. He has pioneered and copyrighted two financial trading systems, *The Profitline Strategy* and *Value Trading,* which are used by his clients investing in mutual funds and stocks.

In addition to rendering investment advice, Mr. Dicks is a principal in Pino & Dicks. The law firm represents investors and brokers nationwide in investment dis-putes and assists companies in public offerings of their securities.

For information about legal and financial services, including his 30-minute Finan-cial Quick Start, phone 1-800-333-3700.

ACKNOWLEDGMENTS

▼

A book like this is only possible with the help of other people. To the following people my special thanks:

Dick Staron, my editor at Macmillan Consumer Information Group, for his insight and assistance in finding good projects.

Sean Casterline, a gifted investment analyst who helped with all the illustrations.

Shielah Constable, who typed so many drafts she's now an expert on mutual funds.

Charles C. Smith, my friend and business partner of fifteen years, for letting me take the time from our business to write this book.

To my wife, Linda, and my daughters, Jennifer and Lindsay, who put up with Dad and his work.

And finally, to my clients, newsletter subscribers, and friends. Thanks for your support and encouragement.

INTRODUCTION

▼

Dear Investor:

In the mid- to late-'80s I was traveling around the country telling people about the advantages of investing in no-load mutual funds. While that wasn't too long ago, very few people who came to the seminars knew much about mutual funds and many people were critical when I said that you could earn 15%–20% annualized returns. Some people were even mad at me when they "tried" mutual funds for six months and didn't make the 15%–20% return. A few of these people even wrote the media criticizing my comments about mutual funds. Unfortunately, these people heard only what they had wanted to hear. I never said and still would never say that in every economy you can jump into mutual funds, or any other investment for that matter, and immediately make 15%–20% returns. Investing is a process, and if you can't give it more than six months then you're not investing, you're gambling.

Investing wasn't the media darling in the mid-'80s like it is today. There wasn't any CNBC. *Kiplinger Magazine* was still *Changing Times,* and if *Money Magazine* was around, it was just getting started. I felt I had to prove myself just so people could see that it could be done. Consequently, in late 1989 I started publishing the *Mutual Fund Advisor*, my newsletter for mutual fund investors. My goal was to show people how to earn a 15%–20% annualized return from investing in mutual funds. I published the newsletter every month and included a Model Portfolio so everyone could see buys and sells. I even calculated the running return so people could follow the numbers and didn't just have to take my word for it. What were the results? From October, 1991 to October, 1996, the Model Portfolio produced an average annual return of 20.17% using no-load mutual funds. The *Mutual Fund Advisor* and Model Portfolio proved that anyone could start investing in mutual funds and, over time, produce the 15%–20% annualized returns I had promoted. (If you would like to see the results yourself, I'll be happy to send a copy of the newsletter at no charge if you call 1-800-333-3700.) No, you can't invest tomorrow and automatically make these types of returns in a short period of time because that would be totally dependent on lucky timing. To achieve these returns you must learn the strategies in this book and then become a consistent investor. You won't make the high returns every year, but like most things in life, your returns will balance out given time and you will be rewarded for your knowledge and consistency.

I have continued the Model Portfolio and it has enjoyed the bull market we have been in by producing even higher returns. How long will these returns continue? Have you missed the opportunity?

The answer to the first question is, of course, I don't know. No one does. However, after you have finished this book you will learn to spot both when the market is likely to slow down and when you can let your money ride, which will maximize your returns. I will teach you specific market signals to watch so you can exit early. This market has shown great strength and brought in many new investors who don't even know what bad markets are. Hopefully, you will learn to follow my indicators and move safely to money market mutual funds when the time comes.

Have you missed the opportunity to make good money in mutual funds? I don't think so. In fact, I think the next few years will provide people with some real opportunities to build a personal nest egg. Some will wait, wanting to see more proof. I hope you aren't one of them. On the contrary, this book was written to teach you how to take control of your own financial future. It shows you how to invest in what has become America's most popular investment and use it to build financial security.

I believe that the best investor is an educated one. In this book, I will teach you not only the fundamentals of mutual fund investing, but also some advance strategies that few people know or understand. Completing this book will give you the education and the comfort to start a mutual fund investing program. Whether it's managing your 401-K, starting a personal retirement program, or planning for your children's college future, it can all start here. I'm excited about the possibilities ahead and I hope you are, too!

Sincerely,

J. W. Dicks

MUTUAL FUND PRIMER

WHAT WE ARE GOING TO TALK ABOUT IN THIS CHAPTER:

- ▶ How a Mutual Fund Works
- ▶ Eight Advantages to Mutual Fund Investing
- ▶ Three Disadvantages to Mutual Fund Investing

The first chapter of this book makes up a primer for mutual fund investing. Its purpose is to assure that you have the basic fundamentals about mutual fund investing and that you understand how to use them to reach your financial goals. For some of you reading this book, the primer will not be necessary and you can proceed immediately to specific chapters that contain investing strategies designed to increase your investment returns. For others, this chapter can be skimmed to be used as a reminder and a reference tool. Finally, perhaps for many of you, this is your first exposure to mutual funds. For you this chapter is essential to make sure that you have a solid foundation and understanding of exactly how mutual funds operate. The work you do now will pay off later when we explore more sophisticated strategies.

WHAT IS A MUTUAL FUND AND HOW DOES IT OPERATE?

A mutual fund is formed when investors pool their money with other investors who have similar investment objectives. The mutual fund invests the pool of money in a diversified portfolio of stocks or debt securities (notes, bills, bonds) that will achieve the investment objectives of the investor. Mutual funds are attractive because your investment is diversified in a large portfolio of different securities. Because the investment is spread over a portfolio of securities, there is much less risk than there would be with a single investment contained in the portfolio.

As a mutual fund investor, you are not only spared the pain and worry of managing your investments, but you are also spared the worry of maintaining accurate records—a problem that many people tend to have. The mutual fund company assembles all of your records for income tax purposes and provides you and the other shareholders with regular reports that contain information on your transactions. With mutual funds, an investor who wants to remain passive can be kept up to date on his investments by simply walking to his mailbox.

Mutual funds offer a variety of alternatives that you can invest in, including income, growth, aggressive growth, and cash reserve. These diverse offerings are frequently made by the same investment advisor under one mutual fund umbrella that is referred to as a "Mutual Fund Family." The best fund families allow investors to move from one fund in the family to another fund in that family by simply calling a toll-free number. This process is referred to as fund "switching" and is an important feature that a fund should offer in order for you to take advantage of changes in the economic environment.

Dollars & Sense: Use "Mutual Fund Families" to quickly and easily "switch" from one mutual fund to another as the economy or performance of the fund dictates. For example, you are presently invested in a long-term bond fund with an average duration of 25 years. You notice that interest rates are increasing. Because this change will make the bonds of your fund less valuable, you call the mutual fund direct and switch from their bond fund to their money market fund. The money market fund will pay higher dividends as interest rates rise.

To decide whether a mutual fund is right for you, first you must make the decision whether you want to invest directly or indirectly in the stock market. If you get satisfaction out of managing your own investments and personally picking individual stocks that you feel have the greatest opportunity for growth, then perhaps mutual funds are not tailored for your personality. However, if you are like many potential investors with little spare time to devote to your investments, mutual funds will be an attractive alternative. Additionally, for the investor who wants to take on a more active role in the investment process, mutual funds can offer the same type of return potential offered by individual stocks, but because of their structure, automatically reduce some of the risks by providing diversity.

Even if you derive satisfaction from managing your own investments, the diversification aspect of mutual funds should be attractive. Many stock analysts feel that an investor should maintain from five to ten different stocks in order to avoid the downside of being heavily invested in one stock. Mutual funds automatically give you this diversification which also greatly reduces your risk. Additionally, because of the cost of buying individual stocks, a diversified portfolio would require more money than most moderate investors could afford. Mutual funds, with their low-cost minimums, allow most investors to utilize the advantages of diversity.

Dollars & $ense: Use mutual funds to diversify portfolio risk that is normally associated with individual stock and at a fraction of the cost, both in terms of portfolio size requirements and transaction cost.

Another attractive feature of mutual fund investing is that most mutual fund investment companies permit investors to specify that all cash distributions be automatically reinvested in additional fund shares.

Money Talks: Mutual fund distributions (payments to investors) can be made up of the following:

1. Dividends, which are the earnings paid out by the companies in a mutual fund portfolio.
2. Interest payments from bond or money market holdings.
3. Capital gains representing profits on stocks held in the mutual fund. These are called long-term gains if held at least twelve months and short-term gains if held less than twelve months.

The result of this feature is that with most mutual funds, the investment returns can be instantaneously reinvested in order to maximize the principal of compounding. This advantage of automatic reinvestment is not presently available with many individual stocks, although some larger companies have recently begun to offer this option. The forward-thinking companies that are now allowing automatic dividend reinvestment realize the advantage of having small shareholders that grow with the company. The reinvestment programs also offer additional cash flow to the company that would not otherwise be available.

Dollars & Sense: Automatically reinvest your mutual fund dividends to take advantage of dollar-cost averaging and the growth affects of compounding your returns.

Money Talks: Dollar Cost Averaging is a system of making periodic purchases of an investment. By buying at all price levels, your costs will be averaged.

The Advantages and Disadvantages of Mutual Fund Investing

In order to make a final determination whether you want to invest in mutual funds, you should compare the advantages versus the disadvantages of mutual fund investing. (See Table 1.1 for a summary.) First, let's look at some of the advantages.

1. Professional management: Some of the best financial minds in the country manage mutual funds. Many have amassed an impressive track record. A fund manager's full-time job is to maximize the profits of that mutual fund. So, for the price of a minimum investment and a small fee, you can have the very best financial experts in the world working on your account. In some cases, these managers receive salaries and bonuses in the multi-million dollar range of athletic superstars. So, if it makes you feel better, you know at least someone is confident in their ability or they wouldn't have paid them that much money.

2. Diversification: One of the classic investment rules is to maintain diversification, or as my mother always said, "Don't put all of your eggs in one basket." This singular advantage is the central investment philosophy behind mutual funds. Not only does investing in one fund give you instant diversification among twenty to thirty different companies, you can maintain additional diversification of your investment portfolio by investing in several different funds with different objectives. This diversification allows you to participate in the traditional growth offered by the equity markets, but reduces your risk that any one company you might select to invest in would not perform well.

Diversification also helps bond investors reduce the risk of credit worthiness of the borrower. Bond mutual funds allow you to seek higher yields by spreading your risk in a fund with a portfolio of different bonds.

3. Lower investment cost: A small investor is on the bottom of the investment ladder. Therefore, everything costs more. For example, you pay the highest commission (sales charge) when you buy stock and again when you sell your position. As a mutual fund investor, commissions can be totally eliminated. By investing in pure no-load (no commission) funds (see Chapter 2 for a complete explanation), there are no transactions costs, either on the front-end or the back-end of a sale. In addition, because the fund itself is large, it can negotiate extremely low commission charges when the fund purchases the underlying stock portfolio. This savings alone helps improve your overall return.

4. Liquidity: Access to your money at a moment's notice can be extremely valuable. Mutual funds are one of the few investments that give you the opportunity to make big profits, and at the same time, the flexibility to get your cash out instantly if needed. In addition, the procedures for actually getting your money from the fund can be as simple as writing a check on your mutual fund account.

5. Automatic reinvestment of dividends: When you own a stock, dividends are generally sent to you—the shareholder. Normally, you cannot simply reinvest the small dividend. If you do, the commission and transaction cost eat up most of the dividend. In recent years, individual companies have begun to form dividend reinvestment plans for their shareholders, but this has not become mainstream by any means. Mutual funds allow you to reinvest all of your dividends or capital gains earned—no matter how small—and without any transaction costs. Because of this automatic reinvestment, the tremendous power of compounding is working for you at all times.

6. Accounting and asset management: Mutual funds offer tremendous management and accounting systems for investors that take away many of the hassles people normally associate with investing. Within one accounting system you can have check writing, debit cards, discount brokerage, and bond and equity investing. For a monthly fee (around $3.00 per month) you can get all of these services plus an accounting statement that itemizes all bills paid and transaction costs.

7. Market timing: No investment vehicle is right for all phases of the economy and stock markets. Mutual funds allow you to switch your investments from stock funds to bond funds to money market funds or to other equity mutual funds instantly. This timing system allows you to always have your money working for you where you believe it will produce the highest return.

8. Indexing: For those investors who are more passive and seek average yields within the current marketplace, mutual funds offer an opportunity to invest in various market indexes including broad market indexes, such as the Wilshire 5,000 and the Standard & Poor's 500 Stock Index, as well as specific indexes on bonds, international funds and growth funds. (Indexes are simply measurements of a certain group of stocks or bonds.) We will discuss them extensively in Chapter 9.

DISADVANTAGES OF MUTUAL FUNDS

1. Risk: You can lose money. All mutual funds promote the theory that they will outperform their competition. They want you to buy their fund and stay with them during ups and downs in the market. Unfortunately, this is not the way to make big money. Certain funds simply perform better in certain fixed economic conditions. Super-aggressive funds can earn tremendous profits in bull markets (periods of time when the market is in a general upward trend), but likewise, when the general market shifts, they can perform poorly in bear markets (periods of time when the market moves in a general downward trend). The opposite is also true; there are certain funds that perform better in bear markets and actually do not perform as well as other funds during bull markets. Both of these statements confirm that consideration should be given to moving your investments as the market or the fund itself dictates. (See Chapter 11, "The Profitline Strategy.")

2. Investment management: Mutual funds are not management-free. Because of the volatility in many mutual funds, they do require some attention on the investor's part. However, the amount of work is minimal compared to most other investments. Fortunately, an hour a week is probably enough for the average investor, but if you do not watch your investment to some degree, you will later wish you had.

3. Operational cost: This is not a big disadvantage for most mutual funds, because the fees are relatively low and no manager will work for you if they don't get paid. Nevertheless, mutual funds do charge management fees, and an increasingly large number charge marketing fees from .5% to as much as 1% annually. Unfortunately, the increase in various fees is a trend that will continue and probably even rise with the better performing funds. In addition, some funds, such as sector funds, charge entry fees (or low-loads) from 2% to 3% to buy the fund as well as redemption fees of typically 1% in order to sell the fund. Like most costs of investing, supply and demand will determine whether the funds can charge these low-loads. Finally, there are funds that charge full loads (commissions) to buy into them. These commissions can cost you as much as 6% to 7% up front. While you may nevertheless consider a commissioned fund because of its track record, be wary that the cost you are paying is extremely high and there is likely to be a no-load fund available that compares to the commissioned fund in both structure and performance.

Table 1.1 Mutual Fund Investing Summary

Advantages:	Disadvantages:
1. Professional management	1. Risk
2. Diversification	2. Investment management
3. Lower investment cost	3. Operational cost
4. Liquidity	
5. Automatic reinvestment of dividends	
6. Accounting and asset management	
7. Market timing	
8. Indexing	

LET'S REMEMBER THIS:

► Mutual funds provide an easy way to diversify your portfolio.

► Mutual funds are an excellent investment to use dollar cost averaging.

► Mutual funds provide low-cost professional management.

▼

CHAPTER 2

THE 12 CATEGORIES OF MUTUAL FUNDS

WHAT WE ARE GOING TO TALK ABOUT IN THIS CHAPTER:

► The Best Place to Park Your Money Between Investments

► Which Funds Offer Long-Term Growth

► How to Buy Mutual Funds Without a Commission

There are essentially twelve types of mutual funds available today. One could argue that the categories I have selected could be broader or narrower depending on your perspective. Nevertheless, all of the funds can fit into one of the twelve categories and I've fixed that number for our classification. Each of the types that I will explain is designed to meet specific investment objectives. While I have attempted to offer a definition for each type of fund, please understand that one of the unfortunate aspects of mutual funds is that they don't all have common definitions. Consequently, what may be simply labeled as a growth fund with one mutual fund family might well be considered an aggressive growth fund in another mutual fund family. For this reason, I will also explain ways you can look at the fund prospectus (disclosure document) and determine through past performance the volatility of a fund. This will help you determine its aggressiveness. Additionally, I would caution you to read a fund's prospectus carefully in order to see not only the types of risks disclosed by the mutual fund company, but also the specific types of holdings that the fund presently owns. While a list of stocks within a fund's portfolio will not guarantee that they will always maintain those individual stocks within their portfolio, it is a strong indication of the investment philosophy of the present manager.

Money Markets

The first category most people think of when considering mutual funds are the stock funds. Nevertheless, I am mentioning money markets first because I want you to start thinking of them as your initial point of entry with any mutual fund investment. The reason for this is because most investments in stock funds should be done in increments over a period of a couple of weeks. As you are studying the market, the money market fund becomes your holding account. Additionally, the money market fund will be a safe place to retreat to when things get rocky with your stock or bond fund. We will discuss this strategy extensively in Chapter 5.

Almost every fund family will have a money market fund that they will allow you to use as your holding account. Money deposited in these accounts is invested for short periods of time, with the earnings usually compounded daily. Most money market funds permit at least two or three checks to be written on the account every month without additional charges. Some offer an unlimited number of transactions, and may combine this service with bank add-ons such as debit cards, credit cards, centralized accounting, stock loss instructions, etc.

Money market accounts work very much like your savings account or your bank money market account, which took the name from the mutual fund industry. However, unlike a bank or savings and loan, the mutual fund money markets are not federally insured. While that does present some additional risk, it is minimal. To offset some of that risk, mutual fund money markets consistently offer a higher percentage rate than bank money markets.

Mutual fund money market returns are directly related to the rise and fall of interest rates. They are a perfect parking place for your investment dollars. When market indicators warn you to leave the equity (or stock side) of a mutual fund family, you need an immediate safe place to store your funds that will give you a decent return on your money while you are waiting for new opportunities in the marketplace. The mutual fund money market is the perfect answer for that. (See Chapter 5 for complete information about money market accounts.)

**Dollars &
Sense:**
Use money market accounts as a temporary place to park your money between investments in equity or bond funds.

Growth Funds

Growth funds, as their name implies, have capital growth as their objective over steady income. Growth funds accomplish this objective by concentrating on companies that the fund managers believe have an excellent chance for price increases. Some funds try to pick small capitalized companies (small cap) that have great potential while other growth funds will pick more established companies (large cap). Growth funds encourage reinvestment of all dividends, capital gains, and any other earnings to promote the growth within your account.

Growth funds tend to take greater risks with the potential of greater gains. In a bull market, tremendous gains are possible with growth funds. In a bear market or even a flat (level) market, the losses can be great. However, the risk of loss is decreased over individual stock selections because of the diversification advantage of mutual funds. A sharp drop in one or two stocks in a growth fund portfolio may be offset by gains in other stock within the portfolio. Even in light of their more aggressive nature, growth funds should play a major role in your mutual fund selections if you are looking to build your portfolio.

**Dollars &
Sense:**
Use growth funds to build assets for the long term.

Aggressive Growth Funds

The addition of the word "aggressive" to growth funds should give you an immediate hint as to their objective. These funds make no bones about the fact that they are interested in making capital gains. In many cases, they will utilize aggressive, sometimes referred to as speculative, investment tools in order to increase the potential for gain. These tools would include leveraging the funds, using options, and exercising hedging techniques in order to maximize gains. Aggressive growth funds are not for the faint at heart because the volatility of these funds can be great. Additionally, it is likely that these funds will move in cycles by doing well one year and not so well the next. Unfortunately, these funds can become a trap for the investor who tries to capitalize on buying a mutual fund in the top categories each year. The reason is that the volatility of aggressive growth funds frequently has them performing best one year and then, because the economy changes, the investment performance falls substantially the next year.

Dollars & Sense: Use aggressive growth funds in strong markets, but watch them carefully for price volatility.

Income Funds

Mutual funds in this category are geared toward producing the highest dividends and interest. Investors in income funds do not expect huge capital gains, but instead look toward current income. A typical income fund allows you to receive regular payments or you may choose to reinvest in additional shares of the income fund.

Income funds can be of two different types. One type of income fund is based entirely on federal, tax-free income-producing sources such as municipal bonds. Another type of income fund will concentrate on corporate bonds (taxable) or attempt to gain even higher yields by investing in "junk" bonds (lower grade bonds that pay a higher yield because the chance of default is higher). Investors who may be concerned about the types of bonds held in portfolios of a mutual fund are encouraged to read the prospectus carefully and determine the type of bond that a particular fund is likely to hold. A bond fund whose name has the words "high yield" in it is conveying a strong indicator that the fund will have at least some combination of bonds which are considered to be junk bonds. It should be noted, however, that even though the term "junk" is used, these particular bonds may play a part in one's investment portfolio in order to achieve a higher yield. The important point is to understand what you're getting into so that you can adjust the percentage of your ownership in that particular fund compared to your overall investment strategy.

Dollars & Sense: Use funds with a blend of high-rated and lower-rated bond funds to diversify both income and risk.

Growth/Income, Equity/Income, and Balanced Funds

As the name implies, growth/income funds have as their objective both current income through dividends and investment accumulation, plus growth through capital appreciation. These objectives will be expressed in their prospectuses. Typically, these funds invest in common stocks that pay dividends. They may also invest in preferred stocks and bonds.

Equity/income funds are similar to the growth/income funds except there tends to be less consideration for growth. Consequently, you usually see less common stock and more preferred stock. There is a very fine line between these two, which is crossed all the time. To really be sure you will have to either read the prospectus or talk with the fund representative to determine the actual makeup. In this category particularly, you can't just buy on the name and be absolutely sure you are getting exactly what you wanted.

If you are a more conservative investor, growth/income funds will be attractive because they offer greater stability and their value does not normally fluctuate as dramatically as growth or aggressive growth funds. Because these funds have a growth aspect to them, they are considered a greater hedge against inflation.

One type of growth/income fund is referred to as a balanced fund. Some people might have made this a separate category, but I decided against this. The reason is because they are just a type of growth/income funds that invests in both common stocks and bonds. Balanced funds differ in that they expressly describe in their prospectuses the exact proportion of their assets that will be placed in stocks and bonds, creating what the manager refers to as the balance. Knowing this distinction helps you pick the fund that meets your own philosophy of balance.

Dollars & Sense: Use growth/income funds to balance your portfolio between income-producing investments and those that offer growth and inflation protection.

SECTOR FUNDS

There are many mutual funds in the marketplace that invest in only one specific industry or area of business, such as banking, insurance, utilities, gold, energy, etc. While the name of the funds generally states the industry in which they specialize, the prospectus of these funds specifically expresses their area of concentration.

The purpose of a sector fund is to allow investors who believe that they have either unique information or a specific ability to analyze a particular industry to take advantage of trends in that industry and still maintain the value of diversity over selecting an individual stock. For example, because of his own personal background, a doctor who is active in the medical field may know that the medical industry is growing at a rapid rate and would expect the stocks within that industry to do well. Instead of attempting to pick the particular stock that will be the leader of the industry, this professional can pick a sector fund that specializes in medical stocks, allowing the doctor to diversify throughout the medical industry.

Another way to use sector funds is to invest in them based on economic cycles. For example, as the economy heats up and inflation becomes a problem, gold or precious metal funds will probably do well because gold has traditionally served as a hedge against inflation. (See Chapter 12 for a complete explanation of sector funds.)

Dollars & Sense: Use sector funds to take advantage of specialized knowledge in an industry.

INTERNATIONAL, GLOBAL, AND OVERSEAS FUNDS

The investment world is becoming more global in nature. Consequently, more opportunities are presenting themselves for investors outside the U.S. than ever before. These opportunities not only include investing in other developed nations, but also opportunities in emerging nations, who have tremendous opportunities for growth, although they are more speculative. Because of the increased awareness of these opportunities available overseas, almost every major fund family in the United States now offers some sort of overseas fund. For a detailed discussion on the opportunities available, see Chapter 14 on global and international investing strategies.

Dollars & Sense: Use global and overseas funds to take advantage of world economics.

BOND FUNDS

Bond funds have already been mentioned in the broader category of income funds. Here, I simply isolated them to remind you that they are a specialty unto themselves. Traditionally, bond funds are divided into categories based on their maturity (pay-off date) and rating. The maturity categories are short term (1 to 5 years), intermediate (5 to 15 years) and long term (15 to 30 years). The rating category, which is done by one of several major rating services, is awarded a designation by letter. The Moody Bond Rating Service awards the best bonds based on safety, AAA. Their lowest rating is D, which signifies a junk bond. These ratings are extremely helpful to investors seeking to determine the potential for a default on the bonds. Such a default could occur when the borrower missed a payment or for some reason refused to pay. This type of information will be disclosed in the prospectus of the fund.

Bond funds are further divided into two major categories: taxable and tax-free. Depending on your marginal tax bracket, you may be better off in a tax-free bond fund even though the yield on a taxable bond would be higher.

WHAT IS YOUR TAX BRACKET?

Your tax bracket is the percentage of money that you pay on your last dollar earned. It is also referred to as your "marginal tax rate."

According to the tax rates for various income levels, we see that a married couple filing a joint return on $50,000 of income would pay 15% on the first $38,000 worth of income and 28% on everything after that. Therefore, they would be said to be in the 28% tax bracket.

The significance of your tax bracket is in knowing how much you will pay in taxes on the next dollar earned or how much you will save in taxes if your next income is not taxable. This analysis enables an investor to determine whether or not a taxable investment with a higher return is as good for him as a tax-free investment in something like a municipal bond that has tax-free income.

For example, an investor in the 36% tax bracket is looking at a $10,000 taxable bond investment that offers a 9% return. Another available option is a tax-free bond at 6.7%. To determine which return is better you would reduce the earnings of the 9% yielding bond by the amount of taxes (9% − 36% = 6.75). Thus, based solely on the return, the taxable bond is slightly better.

Bond funds are traditionally considered more conservative than stock funds. This label should not be confused with the fact that you can lose money in a bond fund just as easily as you can with a stock fund. However, this fact is sometimes lost on investors who buy government-guaranteed Ginnie Maes or Treasury Securities and lose principle when they sell the fund because interest rates have risen since the purchase. A long-term bond can lose 10% of its value with even a 1% rise in rates. Because interest rates are no longer as stable as they once were, bonds can become a high-risk investment and many people aren't even aware of it. To succeed in your investment in bond funds, you need to allocate a portion of your money across the spectrum of funds based on their categories and the direction of interest rates. (See Chapter 7, "How to Pick the Best Bond Fund.")

Index Funds

Index funds do not invest in individual stocks or bonds. Instead, they invest in a particular index made up of either stocks or bonds. These index funds allow you to further diversify your investment and reduce the risk of buying the more narrow selection of stocks typified by your average fund. Some professionals feel that the index funds offer investors a simplified way to participate in mutual fund investing and decrease some of the risk at the same time. (See Chapter 9 for a complete discussion on index funds.)

No-Load Funds vs. Load Funds

When comparing no-load funds and load funds, almost everyone's initial reaction is that load (commissioned) funds must be better than no-load (no commission) funds if they are able to charge something to you for investing in them. However, studies show that this is not true. Loaded funds are no better or worse per se than no-load funds. The important point to be made here is that load funds do not significantly perform better, so there is no reason to pick them over a no-load fund. Do not select a fund simply because it is no-load. On the other hand, given two very similar funds, pick the no-load fund first because you are saving a substantial commission at the start of the transaction. Simple math will show you if you buy two similar funds, one with no commission and one with a 6% commission, you will have to earn a 6% return on the second fund just to get even with the first. That's quite a disadvantage to start off your investment.

Dollars & Sense:

THE NO-LOAD EXAMPLE: A novice invests or buys in a new mutual fund from his local bank that has a 6% load fund. During the first year, it has a great year and returns 20%. Unfortunately, the net yield drops back to 14% because of the load. Not a bad yield, but the load was certainly a lot to make up. If the investor has to switch funds in order to maintain the yield and he doubles up on the commission, 6% on the first fund and 6% on the second fund, the yield for the year now drops to 8%. Add a 2% management fee charged by the fund and you net only 6%. You can now see why you're not making any money.

If instead of using loaded funds, you had used no-load funds and switched funds within a fund family that doesn't charge a commission, your yield would have been

20% less a 1% management fee for a 19% effective yield. The result of this brief exercise will show you quickly why no-load funds have proliferated throughout the marketplace and why loads and management fees are important to your overall return

Dollars & Sense: Use no-load funds to lower your cost of investing.

OPEN END MUTUAL FUNDS

Open end mutual funds are the predominant type of funds in our marketplace. With open end mutual funds, the total number of shares authorized is greater than the number of shares outstanding (already purchased). The public is sold new shares continuously and the fund is always considered to be in the distribution phase. Consequently, federal securities regulators require the fund's prospectuses to be provided with each and every sale of shares.

When you sell your open end mutual fund, they are redeemed at the net asset value (NAV). The redeemed shares are then cancelled. Therefore, selling shares decreases the overall pool of assets while buying into an open end mutual fund increases the pool of assets. When you buy into an open end mutual fund, you receive brand new, previously unissued shares. The significance to this arrangement is that unlike stock, an open end mutual fund does not go up or down in value based on the perception of the value the public has on that mutual fund. Instead, it increases or decreases in value in direct proportion to its underlying assets, the stock in its portfolio.

CLOSED END FUNDS

Closed end mutual funds operate exactly the opposite from open end funds. Closed end funds issue a certain number of shares during an offering just like a new company selling its stock. After completion of the offering, the number of shares outstanding does not change. If you invest in a closed end fund and wish to sell your shares, you would do so in the same manner that you would sell any corporate stock in the marketplace. The price you receive is dependent upon the demand for that particular fund. Therefore, the purchase or the subsequent sale of closed end funds does not effect the pool of assets because money changes hands between fund holder and buyer, not between the fund and investor. The fund maintains its same holdings.

Many people believe that there is an advantage to buying closed end mutual funds because they are frequently sold at a discount. However, the initial discount is due to the fact that when the initial offering of the fund was made, a commission and expenses of the offering were charged. After the offering, the individual share price tends to gravitate toward the true value of the overall portfolio, which will be less the amount that was paid for the commission and the expenses of the offering. Consequently, the real lesson that should be learned from this is not that buying a closed end fund at a discount offers any particular value. Instead, keep in mind that buying a closed end fund during the initial offering stage represents a poor value because based on historical performance, once the offering is over, the fund's value will decrease based on the amount of the commission and the expenses of the offering.

Dollars & Sense: Never buy a closed end fund at its initial offering because you will immediately lose value based on the cost of the offering.

Let's Remember This:

- ▶ Not all mutual funds have the same objective.

- ▶ Understanding a mutual funds investment category will help you make the right selection according to your needs.

- ▶ Mutual funds give every investor a wide choice of investment options.

WHICH TYPE OF MUTUAL FUND MATCHES YOUR NEEDS?

WHAT WE ARE GOING TO TALK ABOUT IN THIS CHAPTER:

- ► How to Pick the Best Mutual Fund
- ► How to Plan Your Own Investment Goals
- ► How to Measure Your Risk Tolerance

Now that you have a better idea about what types of mutual funds are available to you, it is time to consider the hard part, the transition from theory to actually sending your money to the fund itself. The first time you do it will seem a bit cumbersome. You will need to get a prospectus of the fund you select. Then, fill out the paperwork and actually cross the investment barrier by mailing a check. Believe me, it gets a lot easier after the first time, so just do it quickly and get it over with. Procrastination is frequently one of the major differences between successful investors and investor "wanna-bes."

Techniques for Choosing the Right Mutual Fund

The first step in choosing the right mutual fund involves the evaluation of your financial goals. Until you consider your investment goals and objectives, choosing a mutual fund is premature. Once you narrow your objectives, which are directly related to your individual financial goals, your current assets and your risk tolerance, then you can focus on the mutual fund plans that have the same objectives as yours. In order to pick the right mutual fund you must look at three things:

1. Your financial goals;

2. Your current assets and liabilities; and

3. Your risk tolerance.

What Are Your Financial Goals?

Financial goals relate to a great extent to your age. The young couple married at twenty-five will have a long-term view of investing compared to the retired couple, both of whom are 70 years old.

The young couple should not be concerned about earning current income from these investments and can certainly afford to take more risk with their money than the retired couple. Even if the younger couple's investments lost everything, it is one thing to start over at 25 or 30 and it is quite another to start over at 70 or 75.

In my experience of working with retired couples, I find that their main concern is income and safety. Their main fear is that they will outlive their money and that health problems could cause a change in their lifestyle. From an investment standpoint, these financial goals will equate to a more careful allocation of their assets. While they must have enough growth-oriented investments to stay even with inflation, most retired couples want the income from their investments to maintain their standard of living. Because the retired individual has less opportunity to recover from a loss, they should exercise greater care in the selection of their investment. While this could lead to lack of action as a result of fear, it should lead to greater involvement and understanding. The retired individual has more time to spend with their investment than most other age brackets. This extra time should be spent gaining knowledge about how to handle the investments. Doing so could lead to a successful and rewarding job of caring for your finances and protecting your future.

The younger couple does not have greater concerns in magnitude, but they probably have more in number. In addition to trying to increase their standard of living, other goals that have great importance for a young couple include savings for a home, having a family, and starting a college fund. The tendency is to want to do everything now. In reality, this defeats the purpose of planning. Each goal has its own special set of circumstances that you can take advantage of by planning properly. For example, you may decide to compromise on college by setting aside enough money for your child to go to an in-state public college or university as opposed to a private one. This one decision makes a dramatic difference in how much money you will ultimately need and consequently, how much present money needs to be set aside. Having made this decision may now open the door to saving for a down payment on a home. Here again, you need to answer certain threshold questions. How big a house do you want? What is the average price for that size house? How large of a loan can you qualify for? How much down payment will you need? All of these questions are planning issues that must be answered before you can expect to know how much to save or what type of investment will be the best.

Whatever your age or position in life, you must go through the process of evaluating your goals and determining your financial objectives for the future. Above all, you also must be honest with yourself. I've sat across from investors who told me with an absolutely straight face that they had to have a 14% return in order to have the lifestyle on which they insisted. However, they also added, they could not risk losing any principal. I told them and I'm telling you, these are incompatible objectives. You cannot get higher returns without corresponding higher risk. Yet time and time again, investors tell their advisors and themselves that is what they want. This unrealistic approach to investing will only set you up for frustration and failure.

**Dollars &
Sense:** Set honest and realistic financial goals and readjust them periodically as your life needs change. To cement the goals in your mind, write them down and commit to them.

WHAT ARE YOUR CURRENT ASSETS AND LIABILITIES?

In order to meet your goals, take the time to determine your current financial status and set a realistic course for where you want to be with your investments. If you find that you will be unable to meet your objectives, don't despair or hide from the truth either. Plan accordingly or change your plans. Maybe you'll find that to reach your financial objective you will have to get a part time job and contribute 100% of that money to your retirement. You may not want to do that, but at least you'll know your choice. Not long ago I sat down with a young couple frustrated about their financial condition. They were heavily in debt. Both were working and each had reached a feeling of desperation. They had come to me seeking an answer. How could they ever solve their financial problems? The answer was simple. It wasn't what they wanted to know, but it was simple. They had two choices: Make more or spend less. Was the couple happy with my suggestion? No. They had no idea what their financial goals were. They didn't understand their current financial condition and yet they wanted to start investing today. For some reason, they either would not or could not come to the realization that paying down their high credit card debt of 18% to 21% was a way of investing. It wasn't a mutual fund, but it provided a great return.

No matter how much I want you to put into practice all of the ideas in this book, you should not start investing until you have your current financial house in order. It makes no sense to open up a mutual fund investment account until you've paid off your credit cards that have interest rates from 18% to 21%. If you pay off those credit cards first, you've guaranteed yourself the same 18% to 21% return on your money. No one can guarantee you that in mutual funds.

Studying your assets and liabilities may also show you other areas where your finances need attention before you should consider starting an investment program. For example, your company may offer a corporate stock purchase program on a payroll deduction plan. Frequently, the companies match your funds or at least a portion. If you are comfortable with your comprehensive growth potential, this type of program should be strongly evaluated because the matching funds offered by the corporation far exceed likely returns in an individual's own investment. While we are on the subject of corporate savings plans, make sure you have also maximized any retirement program first before you start a separate investment plan. Company 401-K, tax-deferred savings plans are always preferred over individual savings accounts.

Dollars & Sense:

Before you invest:

1. Pay off all high interest rate credit cards.

2. Participate in any matching funds savings programs available through your corporation.

3. Start a retirement program: IRA, Keough, SEP, 401-K, or 403-B.

To help in this assessment of your assets and liabilities, at the end of this chapter I have included a copy of my company's Personal & Financial Profile for you to complete. Take the time to fill it out. Use it as a road map to see where your finances are currently and to help you understand where you want to go. (See worksheet at the end of the chapter.) Many of our clients are amazed when they complete the profile to actually see their total financial picture. Although it may be hard to understand, some people don't realize all the debts they have or that they had money sitting in an unproductive CD or money market. Too often a big discovery is that the spouse has different goals than they do. Completing this form together with your mate will give you the opportunity to openly discuss financial issues that may have been put aside for another day or perhaps even avoided. Be honest with yourselves and speak openly about your plans and dreams. Completing this form can be a terrific opportunity to understand your finances and make specific plans for the future. If you feel you need individual help, call my office about our 30-minute Financial Quick Start. We'll be happy to discuss our personalized program to get you started on the road to success. For information, call 1-800-333-3700.

On the second to last page of the form is a place to rank objectives on a scale of 1-10. Don't simply put 10 for all of them; go through each and evaluate their importance. If you are a couple, it is fun to do this separately and then compare notes. You may find out some interesting things about your spouse you didn't know and why you have disagreed with each other about money in the past. If your spouse lists "safety of capital" as a 10 and you put it as a 1 or 2, you can imagine the problem this will cause if your investment selections ever lose money. In my law firm, we work with people who have lost money in investments and try to help them recover. I've had grown men almost break down because they didn't want to tell their wife about an investment they made that lost money. In one case, the man decided not to pursue recovery of his lost investment because he would have had to explain it to his wife.

Although you may scoff at the inevitable truth you discover about an investment program, the simple fact is that there is always a direct ratio between risk and reward. If you are unwilling or unable to take a risk of your principal, that's fine. Just admit it and understand that your reward (return) will have less potential than that of a person willing to lose all or even some of his principal. You, the conservative investor, may ultimately do better than the active investors willing to accept risk because they may lose principal. On the other hand, by taking the conservative approach you have guaranteed yourself a loss of opportunity to do better. Whatever your decision, make sure your investment solutions are consistent with that decision. If you decide you can't risk principal loss, don't invest in high risk securities.

What is Your Risk Tolerance?

Mutual funds carry risk. You will recall me telling you about investors who demand high returns with no risk. I stated that this was an incompatible objective—and it is. Like I told these investors, you too must understand your risk tolerance. If you cannot risk the loss of principal, you cannot invest in equity funds because inevitably they will go down in value at one time or another. While some advisors would refer this type of individual to bond funds, this too could be a mistake. Depending on the type of bond fund and its maturity, makeup principal can certainly be at risk. For example, a thirty-year bond portfolio will lose approximately 10% of its value for every 1% rise in interest rates. That doesn't seem very conservative to me. Instead, a person who can't lose principal may want to consider putting a large portion of their investment in individually selected short-term, high-grade bonds. The short-term quality will reduce the bond portfolio's sensitivity to interest rate charges and allow you to simply hold the bond to maturity and be assured of your principal. The high-grade quality will decrease default possibilities to acceptable risk tolerance. You can accomplish much of the same with a short-term bond fund, but because the fund is always reinvesting in new bonds with changing maturities, you will have some fluctuations in principal. In a rising interest rate environment, this fluctuation is greatly minimized over time because the portfolio is being replaced with higher interest rate bonds.

Money Talks: Risk is a word that means different things to different people. Therefore, if anyone ever asks you about your risk tolerance, you need to find out what they mean. For example, while most people think of risk as "market risk" (loss due to price fluctuations), there is also inflation risk, tax risk, volatility risk, and time value risk.

Can You Minimize Mutual Fund Risk?

The answer to this question is "yes." The reason is because although we know that mutual funds carry risk, it is a calculated one. By this I mean that while certain funds have higher risk than others, it is only in comparison to each other as opposed to comparison between mutual funds and other forms of investment that may have even higher risks. For example, an aggressive growth fund has more risk than a growth fund and both tend to have more risks than an income/growth fund. However, this increased risk is not nearly as great as comparing the income/growth fund to buying futures, naked options, diamonds or any number of other high risk investments outside the mutual fund arena. Fortunately, there is also an easy way to help determine the risk of a particular mutual fund before you invest and specific strategies to reduce your risk. (For further information, see Chapter 8, "Strategies to Reduce Your Risk.")

PERSONAL & FINANCIAL PROFILE

PERSONAL DATA

Last Name _____ First Name _____ Spouse Name _____

Mailing Address _____

Phone (___) _____

NAME	AGE	DATE OF BIRTH	HEALTH	OCCUPATION	SOCIAL SECURITY #
Client					
Spouse					
Children					
Other Dependents					

OCCUPATION

Employer (Client) _____ Years _____

Address _____ Phone (_____) _____

Employer (Spouse) _____ Years _____

Address _____ Phone (_____) _____

CONSULTANTS	NAME	ADDRESS	PHONE

Accountant _____

Attorney _____

Banker _____

Insurance Broker _____

Other _____

INCOME AND TAXATION

Current Annual Gross Income	Client	Spouse	19___ Year Total	19___ Year Total
Salary, Fees, Bonuses, etc.	$	$	$	$
Interest	$	$	$	$
Dividends	$	$	$	$
Real Estate	$	$	$	$
Other	$	$	$	$
Total Adjusted Gross Income	$	$	$	$
Deductions			$	$
Taxable Income			$	$
Total Estimated Monthly Expenses, Not Including Taxes or Investments				$

TAX RETURN SUMMARY

Last 4 Years	19_____	19_____	19_____	19_____
Adjusted Gross Income	$	$	$	$
Taxable Income	$	$	$	$
Tax Liability - Federal	$	$	$	$
Tax Liability - State	$	$	$	$

ASSETS AND LIABILITIES

Liquid Asset Group	Amount	Bank or Company	Maturity	Interest %
Cash (On Hand)	$			
Checking	$			
Checking	$			
Savings	$			
Savings	$			
Certificates of Deposit	$			
Certificates of Deposit	$			
Certificates of Deposit	$			
Credit Union	$			
Credit Union	$			
T-Bill	$			
Other	$			

EMPLOYEE BENEFITS

Type of Company Plan	Retirement Age	Retirement Benefits	Voluntary Contributions	Current Value	Death Benefit Now	% Vested
Pension		$	$	$	$	
Profit Sharing		$	$	$	$	
Savings		$	$	$	$	
Tax Shelter Annuity		$	$	$	$	

RETIREMENT PLANS

Type	Current Value	Vested Value	Beneficiary	How Vested	Where Held
IRA	$	$			
Keogh	$	$			
Corporate	$	$			
Other	$	$			
Other	$	$			

OTHER ASSETS

Asset	Market Value	Loan Balance	Asset	Market Value	Loan
Automobile	$	$	Boat	$	$
Automobile	$	$	Art	$	$
Automobile	$	$	Gems	$	$
Furniture	$	$	Precious Metals	$	$
Jewelry	$	$	Miscellaneous	$	$

LIFE INSURANCE

Company	Type	Date Acquired	Insured	Owner	Beneficiary	Face Value	Cash Value	Loans	Annual Premium
						$	$	$	$
						$	$	$	$
						$	$	$	$
						$	$	$	$
						$	$	$	$

MEDICAL AND DISABILITY INSURANCE

Type	Insurer	Insured	Benefits	Premium	Paid by Whom
Disability Income			$	$	$
Hospitalization			$	$	$
Major Medical			$	$	$
Other			$	$	$

NOTES RECEIVABLE

From Whom	Amount	Monthly Payments	Interest %	Due Date	Collateral
	$	$			
	$	$			
	$	$			

SECURITIES   *(If more space is necessary, please attach an additional sheet.)*

Stock or Bond	Number of Shares	Date Acquired	Purchase Price	Market Value	Margin of Loans	Annual Cash Flow
			$	$	$	$
			$	$	$	$
			$	$	$	$

Name of Fund						
			$	$	$	$
			$	$	$	$
			$	$	$	$

ANNUITIES

Name of Company	Amount	Date Acquired	Maturity Date	Interest %	Title Held
	$				
	$				

REAL ESTATE

Address	Description	Market Value	Total Loans	Purchase Price	Date Acquired	Annual Cash Flow	Title Held
		$	$	$		$	
		$	$	$		$	
		$	$	$		$	
		$	$	$		$	
		$	$	$		$	

PARTNERSHIP INTERESTS

Name of Organization	Business Activity	Percent Ownership	Market Value	Initial Investment	Client's Annual Cash Flow	Title Held
			$	$	$	
			$	$	$	
			$	$	$	
			$	$	$	

LOANS OUTSTANDING

Type	Original Amount	Current Balance	Interest %	No. of Payments Until Paid
Automobile	$	$		
Master Card/Visa				
Department Store				
Unsecured Bank Loan				
Student Loan				
Other				

PRIORITIES AND NEEDS SURVEY

Please rate the importance of the following objectives as they relate to your financial plan. One (1) is the least important; ten (10) is the most important.

1. Income Tax Deferral/Relief	1	2	3	4	5	6	7	8	9	10
2. Review Insurance Needs & Premiums	1	2	3	4	5	6	7	8	9	10
3. Budgeting	1	2	3	4	5	6	7	8	9	10
4. Inflation Protection	1	2	3	4	5	6	7	8	9	10
5. Diversification of Investments	1	2	3	4	5	6	7	8	9	10
6. Capital/Equity Growth	1	2	3	4	5	6	7	8	9	10
7. Current Income Production	1	2	3	4	5	6	7	8	9	10
8. Safety of Capital	1	2	3	4	5	6	7	8	9	10
9. Liquidity	1	2	3	4	5	6	7	8	9	10
10. Financial Independence	1	2	3	4	5	6	7	8	9	10
11. Retirement Planning	1	2	3	4	5	6	7	8	9	10
12. Freedom from Money Management	1	2	3	4	5	6	7	8	9	10
13. Estate Planning	1	2	3	4	5	6	7	8	9	10
14. Investment Analysis	1	2	3	4	5	6	7	8	9	10
15. Other	1	2	3	4	5	6	7	8	9	10

PLEASE LIST YOUR PERSONAL GOALS AND OBJECTIVES

1. IMMEDIATE GOALS:

2. SHORT-TERM GOALS:

3. LONG-TERM GOALS:

INVESTMENT EXPERIENCE
Indicate the frequency of your Investment in marketable securities.

_____ Often   _____ Occasionally   _____ Seldom   _____ Never

TAX SHELTER INVESTMENT HOLDINGS INCLUDING LIMITED PARTNERSHIPS:

Name of Investment	Year Purchased	Approximate Amount

INVESTMENT OBJECTIVES

Are you associated with or employed by another NASD broker-dealer? _____ Yes _____ No

Have you previously purchased a private securities offering? _____ Yes _____ No

To the best of my (our) information and belief, the information supplied by me (us) is true and correct in all respects.

_____   _____
Date   Customer Signature

_____   _____
Date   Customer Signature

                                    _____
                                    (Print Name)

                                    _____
                                    (Print Name)

INVESTMENT ADVISORY REPRESENTATIVE

_____   By _____
Date   Signature

SUPERVISOR ACCEPTANCE

_____   By _____
Date   Principal's Signature

LET'S REMEMBER THIS:

► In order to make your best investment you must understand your own investment goals.

► Risk is an element of every investment and successful investors pick funds that fit their risk tolerance.

► Time spent taking personal inventory is time well spent.

CHAPTER 4

How to Set Up a Mutual Fund Account

What We Are Going to Talk About in This Chapter:

- ► The Best Ways to Invest in a Mutual Fund
- ► How to Use Mutual Fund Networks to Your Advantage
- ► Recommended Fund Families and How to Use Them to Your Advantage

There are basically four ways to invest in a mutual fund, as explained below. As you would expect, they each have their own advantages and disadvantages. You must ultimately pick the one that best fits your needs. That choice may or may not be the cheapest. One size does not fit all, no matter what the mass marketers would have you believe.

1. Buy direct from the mutual fund company. Major mutual funds have their own marketing departments that work with investors through toll-free numbers. These funds offer their products in a low-commission or no-commission (no-load) basis. When the mutual fund investment company offers a group of funds it is called a "fund family." Within the fund family are different types of funds. For example, Invesco Funds Group is a fund family. The company has a growth fund, balanced funds, bond funds and even sector funds.

Table 4-1   Invesco Funds Group Mutual Fund Family
P.O. Box 173706
Denver, CO 80217-3706
1-800-525-8085

INVESCO Asian Growth	INVESCO Pacific Basin
INVESCO Balanced	INVESCO Multi-asset Allocation
INVESCO Dynamics	INVESCO Select Income
INVESCO Emerging Growth	INVESCO Short-term Bond
INVESCO European	INVESCO Small Company
INVESCO European Small Company	INVESCO Strategic Energy
INVESCO Financial Services	INVESCO Strategic Environmental Services
INVESCO Growth	INVESCO Strategic Gold
INVESCO Health Sciences	INVESCO Strategic Leisure
INVESCO High Yield	INVESCO Strategic Technology
INVESCO Income U.S. Government Securities	INVESCO Strategic Utilities
	INVESCO Tax-free Intermediate Bond
INVESCO Industrial Income	INVESCO Tax-free Long-term Bond
INVESCO Intermediate Government Bond	INVESCO Value Trust Equity
	INVESCO Value Trust Total Return
INVESCO International Growth	INVESCO Worldwide Capital Goods
INVESCO Latin America Growth	INVESCO Worldwide Communications

There are many reasons you may select a particular fund family and they all try to position themselves with different niches. For example, Fidelity Funds has over 116 funds within its family. You will almost always see one of Fidelity's funds in the top 10. Because they have so many, at least one will perform well in every type of market. (See Table 4-3 for a list of their funds.)

Vanguard Funds Group (1-800-662-7447) is another example of a well-run and highly successful fund family. Their claim to fame centers around lower costs and they consistently meet this objective. Obviously, all things being equal, lower cost to the investor means a higher return.

The key to selecting a fund family is not just based on the number of funds they have, nor the cost. You also want to be sure that they offer a variety of types. For example, Benham Funds (1-800-331-8331) has one of the best selections of bond funds, particularly zero bond funds. On the other hand, it is not known for sector funds or international funds. And if you want to invest in one of these markets, you will have to open an additional account somewhere else.

Retirement account availability is also important in picking a fund. You want low-cost or no-fee retirement accounts with minimal restrictions. The major funds all seem to be very competitive in this area because retirement programs are extremely important for their longevity.

Additional information that you should obtain from the mutual fund investment company includes minimum investment requirements, transaction cost to change from one fund to another, and availability of telephone switching. Is the fund available during the hours you are interested in investing? You should inquire about check writing privileges, costs of the service, and the type of reporting they provide. It may not seem important now but come tax time, the readable consolidated statement is one of your biggest friends.

Money Talks: Telephone switching is a method of moving your investment from one fund in the fund family to another by simply calling your investment company. The advantage of this service is that you can move quickly from one fund to another as changes in the market or the specific fund dictate.

2. **Full-service stock brokerage firm.** If you buy a mutual fund from a full-service brokerage firm, then you are going to pay a commission. The issue you need to consider is whether or not the broker is earning his pay. If he is, don't begrudge his commission no matter what the financial media says about avoiding commissions when you invest. On the other hand, if the broker doesn't earn the fee, why pay it? As we said before, statistics have clearly shown that there is no correlation between a fund being successful and your having to pay a commission to buy it. If anything, the opposite may be true. Nevertheless, if you are a novice, you may need to pay for help in the beginning, but just make sure the help you are getting is worthwhile. Once you are able to select your own funds then you can save on the commissions.

3. **Discount broker.** Discount brokerage firms have attempted to carve out a special niche in the mutual fund business. These brokerage companies have gone directly to the mutual fund investment companies and arranged to be

their marketing arm in exchange for a percentage of the management fee the fund charges. In return, the discount broker offers all of the funds to their investors as though it were one large fund family. This arrangement allows you to move from one fund family to another with the same ease that you normally have just within the family's own fund. The result is a much broader selection of funds that you can take advantage of and the use of a telephone switching service. Charles Schwab (1-800-435-4000), Fidelity Advisors (1-800-544-8666), and Jack White (1-800-233-3411) are all national discount brokers that offer this service. Each has a different fee structure, and it would be beneficial for you to at least get the information on each of these options. (See Figure 4-1 for more information on these brokerage firms.)

4. Investment Advisors. Investment advisors offer money management services to the individual investor. The money management accounts take all of the services of broker, fund, and advisor and bundle them up into a master account. Investment advisors work directly with you to pick the best funds for you to achieve your financial goals. The company helps you pick the mutual fund, monitors the performance, trades to other funds as the market dictates, and provides a consolidated statement for all your funds. The advantage of this type of company is the service and advice. The disadvantage is the cost. The bottom line for you as an investor is to determine whether a full-time manager can make you more money than you can on your own. The answer will be different based on your own knowledge, experience, and time. If the investment advisor can make you more money, then they are worthwhile. If they can't, then they aren't. It really is as simple as that. If you don't know, then try a test. Give an advisor part of your money to manage and then you can manage an equal part. After a year, it will be easy to see if they were worth their fee.

Reading the Prospectus

The first step in your mutual fund investment process was to select a particular fund or fund family. Once you have narrowed the field, you will want to request a prospectus from the fund itself. Now I realize that most of you would rather dig a ditch than read a prospectus, but they are a very important step in your investment process.

Figure 4-1   Discount Brokers Operating Mutual Fund Networks

Charles Schwab & Company, Inc.
101 Montgomery Street
San Francisco, CA 94104
(800) 435-4000

Schwab's no-load, no transaction fee program is called the *Schwab OneSource Program.* The program consists of 70 families and over 548 no-load funds. The OneSource program consists of major fund families but also has many new fund families available.

Charles Schwab has set a short-term trading restriction on the mutual funds within the program. The investor is required to hold the mutual fund for a minimum of 90 days. If the fund is sold within 90 days of purchase (termed a short-term redemption), the investor will pay a transaction fee on the sale (the minimum fee is around $30). If you have 15 short-term redemptions within one year, your account will be coded as a short-term trading account and from that point on, you will be required to pay transaction fees on all sales and purchases.

Fidelity Investments
P.O. Box 770001
Cincinnati, OH 45277
(800) 544-8666

Fidelity Investments' no-load, no transaction fee network is called *Funds Network* and it consists of major fund families but also has a larger number of new fund families.

The Fidelity Funds Network program is unique in that they do not have a set short-term redemption policy. However, Fidelity does adhere to any short-term redemption policy that the mutual fund family may have. Therefore, you may have to still pay a fee if a fund is sold within a short period of time.

Jack White & Co.
9191 Towne Centre Dr., Suite 220
San Diego, CA 92122
(800) 233-3411

Jack White & Co. has a no-load, no transaction fee mutual fund program which they refer to as their *No Fee Network.* The network consists of 125 mutual fund families with a total of 815 funds. Jack White & Co. has the largest no-load, no transaction fee network available from the three discount brokers. The program consists of most major no-load families and is continually growing in size. Additionally, the mutual fund minimum investments are lower at Jack White & Co. Therefore, investors who are just starting out may be inclined to use Jack White & Co.

Jack White & Co. has also implemented a short-term trading restriction on the mutual funds within the program. The investor is required to hold the mutual fund for a minimum of 90 days. If the fund is sold within 90 days of purchase (termed a short-term redemption), the investor will pay a transaction fee on the sale (the minimum fee is around $30). If you have 15 short-term redemptions within one year, your account will be coded as a short-term trading account and from that point on, you will be required to pay transaction fees on all sales and purchases.

The prospectus contains all the disclosure you ever wanted to know about a fund and more. It will tell you about the manager, including his experience, investment philosophy, and the fees he will charge. While this information is very important, it is the ministerial information that is probably the most helpful. How do you get your money invested and how do you get it out of the fund when you want to? At this point of the investment, most people are unconcerned about getting out their money. Usually, the rush is to get invested quickly and to take advantage of a market rally. You can believe me now or believe me later, but the additional profit that you may make now will be lost quickly when you are trying to get out of your investment and are delayed by several weeks because you did not take the time to set up your fund properly in the first place. Make sure you save the prospectus in your permanent file so that you will have an immediate reference point when needed.

Dollars & $ense: Request several prospectuses from mutual fund companies and compare them to the points discussed in this chapter.

Other disclosures to review in the prospectus are:

1. **The Fund Investment Advisor and Fees.** Unless you are an experienced investor, the name of the fund advisor probably will not mean much to you. You will, however, be able to use the information from this section to compare advisors' fees. These annual charges vary from .5% to 2% as an extreme. The fund will also disclose whether they charge 12-B-1 fees, which run approximately 1% to 1.5% and are used for marketing the fund to new investors. Also, be cautious of any redemption fees the fund may charge when you sell. Some funds require that you stay invested for a certain period of time. Therefore, if you sell early then you will pay a redemption fee for the privilege.

Money Talks: 12-B-1 fees are built-in marketing fees that some funds charge investors. These fees are used to pay brokerage firms and other investment advisors who sold you the fund. The fees are like hidden commissions because they allow the fund to say it is "no load," but they use these fees to pay the broker. Redemption fees are rear loads on commissions charged when you sell a fund. These fees are used by mutual funds to discourage investors from moving out of their fund family.

2. **Fund Class.** Even when you buy a specific mutual fund, you may be getting a slightly different version than someone else you know who bought the same

fund. The reason is because mutual funds are frequently offered in different classes. If you buy direct from the fund, then you get one class. But if you buy from a full service broker, then you may get another class. The differences between the classes are the cost that the fund charges you for management. For example, Class A shares may have a .95% management fee, Class B shares a 1.25% fee and Class C a 1.5% management fee. While it will appear on the surface that you have purchased the same fund as everyone else, it might cost you as much as .55% more to be in the fund than someone else. Over time, that's a big difference because the fee is charged every year. Very few people know to check for their fund class, but now you do.

3. **Portfolio.** The makeup of the fund will greatly help you in your selection process. By reading what constitutes a particular fund's portfolio, you can determine if it is right for you.

   Mutual funds are very creative about their names. For instance, you won't see the XYZ Junk Bond fund but you will see the XYZ High Yield Fund. The funds realize that investors won't buy a fund that calls itself "junk," but calling one "high yield" is an entirely different matter. Misleading? I'll let you be the judge. What I want you to learn is not to judge a fund by its name, but by its holdings. The only way to really understand its holdings is to read the prospectus and see what it's investing in.

   With the continued expansion of funds, there is truly one fund suited for everyone. The fund can be very diverse, or as in sector funds, specific to certain industries. Making a decision as to what is right for you is a part of the process that should not be omitted.

Dollars & Sense: Funds' portfolios change frequently. Consequently, before you invest, feel free to contact the fund directly to see the current makeup of its portfolio.

4. **Shareholder Services.** As we have previously discussed, mutual funds offer complete financial accounting for their customers. The services are helpful and reasonably priced. Feel free to contact the mutual fund's investor representative. They are available by way of toll-free numbers to answer your questions and help you with your account. While I have never had trouble with a representative, if you find one to be uncooperative, then immediately ask for his or her supervisor. You will find they are ready and willing to help.

Once you invest with the fund, continue to work with the investor representatives to get more information about the changing conditions of the fund. Remember, you pay the investor representative's salary with the management fee, so use the service.

Dollars & Sense: One service that you may want to inquire about early on is tax service. Some funds and discount brokerage companies will do all of your capital gains and loss calculations for you. This is a big time-saver and reduces your accounting bill.

5. **How to Purchase.** All prospectuses provide brief summaries on how to invest your dollars. It is here that you will find information on minimum purchase amounts, increment investing, and specialty investing like retirement accounts and custodial accounts.

You will need to decide how you want your account set up: individual ownership, joint tenants, right of survivorship, tenants in common, trustee or custodian. The method you choose obviously depends upon your circumstances. While the fund representative will not tell you what to do, they are knowledgeable enough to explain the differences and tell you what the various methods of account title will accomplish. If you happen to have a living trust, don't forget to set up your mutual fund account to conform to the name of your trust, indicating the trustee as well. The fund representatives are experienced in this area, so again, don't be afraid to ask.

When you set up your account, use the same name and mailing address for all your account funds. Do not use a nickname for one account or an initial for one and not the other. To avoid any unnecessary bookkeeping errors and misunderstandings, be consistent.

Dollars & Sense: When you set up the mutual fund account, find out the specific feature for redemption. Many funds require written instructions and that your signature be signed under a bank guarantee. That means you must physically sign the fund's redemption request before a bank officer. This is different than a notary public. This process can take several days so I recommend making up a liquidation request form ahead of time, get your signature guaranteed, and keep the form on file until you need to use it. Date it only when you use it.

6. **Start in a Money Market.** When you buy your mutual fund, you may purchase that fund directly. Another alternative is to first place your money in

the fund family's money market fund, then immediately switch into the stock or bond fund of your choice. I recommend this procedure because if you open the money market fund first, then the fund provides a prospectus on that fund and allows you to switch back without a waiting period. This procedure gives you a place to move your money from a stock or bond fund when the market condition falls. You exit into your money market. This will save you days and dollars in a down market if you had to wait to set up your money market fund before you moved out of your other fund. If you invest directly with a fund that does not allow you to move to a money market account, then selling is likely to be time consuming whenever that time comes. In a down market, that could be costly.

RECOMMENDED FUND FAMILIES

Because there are thousands of different types of funds, I have tried to condense your investment search by listing the major fund families and their phone numbers (see Table 4-2). Please call several of them and ask them to send you information on their leading growth, bond, and money market funds. When reading the information and prospectus, look for the key ideas we have discussed in this book. After reviewing this information for a few funds, you'll find that the process and information is similar. And as you get more familiar, you'll also become more comfortable.

Table 4-2   Major Mutual Fund Families

Alger 1-800-992-3863	Evergreen 1-800-807-2940	Invesco 1-800-525-8085
American 1-800-828-5050	Federated 1-800-245-5040	Janus 1-800-525-8983
Benham 1-800-331-8331	Fidelity 1-800-544-8888	Lexington 1-800-526-0057
Berger 1-800-333-1001	Founders 1-800-525-2440	MFS 1-800-637-2929
Columbia` 1-800-547-1707	Gabelli 1-800-422-3554	Nueberger & Berman 1-800-877-9700
Dreyfus 1-800-645-6561	IAI 1-800-945-3863	PBHG 1-800-433-0051

continues

Table 4-2   Major Mutual Fund Families (continued)

Pimco	Scudder	20th Century
1-800-426-0107	1-800-225-2470	1-800-345-2021
Robertson Stephens	SteinRoe	Vanguard
1-800-766-3863	1-800-338-2550	1-800-662-7447
T. Rowe Price	Strong	Warburg Pincus
1-800-638-5660	1-800-368-1030	1-800-257-5614

SELLING YOUR FUND

For most funds, selling or redeeming your shares is very straightforward and can be accomplished with relatively little effort on the part of mutual fund holders. If at all possible, keep your securities with the mutual fund company. Do not take possession. If you do, then you'll have to send the certificates back when you want to sell. Additionally, you'll have to go through the time-consuming process of attaching redemption forms and getting your signature guaranteed by a bank. There is nothing more costly in a declining market than this process. This is what happened to a lot of people in the 1987 crash and they were delayed several weeks. By then, the drop in the market had already happened and selling only assured a loss. Each of these investors sold at precisely the wrong time simply because they weren't prepared. Make sure you can sell your fund position with one phone call or if you can't get through, then find out if they'll accept fax sell orders. Again, all of these precautions are for timing. Hopefully, you won't need to worry about it, but preparation is everything in a disaster.

Dollars & Sense: To avoid delays in selling your funds, don't take actual possession of your securities. Not only does this save time when you sell the fund, it avoids the expense you incur (1%–2%) if you lose your certificates.

First of all, you must realize there are several ways to calculate your mutual fund's performance. There is no universal method of calculation, but some methods more accurately reflect total return. Mutual funds provide quarterly reports that use elaborate charts and graphs to show how the fund performed during the past five years or so, but these reports do not necessarily summarize the period that you need. While mutual funds are barred from making misleading comparisons in their promotional literature by depicting only data from a very productive quarter, they still remain creative in their yield presentations.

New mutual fund investors are often confused by the disparity between what is reported in the newspapers about their fund's performance and what their fund representative has told them. The tables reported in the newspaper list the daily net asset values (NAVs). What is confusing is that, taken alone, these daily figures mean absolutely nothing about the fund's overall performance over a period of time. This may come as a surprise to some of you who thought you were diligently following your fund's performance by reading the paper every day.

However, even if you watched a mutual fund in the newspaper every day for a year and there was very little change in the net asset value, you still could be misled by your observation of the fund's performance during that year. Even though the net asset value did not change very much, the fund probably distributed income dividends and capital gains. Actually, a capital gains distribution tends to decrease the net asset value, because the fund is dispersing money that had previously been included in the fund's assets. Therefore, you cannot get a feel for a fund's true performance unless you take into consideration dividends and capital gains distributions.

To illustrate how calculations can vary depending on which formula you use, let's consider the following hypothetical situation. You purchase Aggressive Growth Fund, a no-load growth mutual fund, at $15 per share net asset value.

Six months later a bullish market has caused Aggressive Growth's net asset value to climb to $20 per share. There is a capital gains distribution of $5 per share, which returns the fund's net asset value to $15. Six months later, the net asset value of the fund is $30, indicating a prosperous year for fund holders. If you simply look on the surface at the price of the fund and do not take into consideration the distribution of capital gains, the fund had an increase of 100% ($15 per share to $30 per share). This method of calculating the fund's total return is not the best method available.

A better method of calculating Aggressive Fund's performance would be to include the $5 capital gains distribution (paid to you in cash or additional shares) in the return calculation. Adding that to the $15 per share increase over the year would give fund holders a 133% increase.

Perhaps the most accurate method of calculating the performance of your fictional mutual fund is to make an assumption that the $5 capital gains distribution was reinvested in Aggressive Growth's portfolio. The $5 capital gains distribution would go back into the fund at a time when the shares had a net asset value of $15 per share, which in effect would give the fundholder one and one-third shares as opposed to just one share at the end of the year. The final net asset value of the fund was $30, but you also have additional shares. This calculation, which takes into consideration the capital gains distribution, would give a total return of 166% over a period of one year.

As you can tell, numbers can be made to tell different stories. Always be sure that you compare apples to apples and don't forget to consider tax ramifications, which haven't even been discussed yet. Whatever method you use, always calculate the total return of your fund taking into consideration all increases and distributions you have received.

Dollars & Sense: When comparing returns on various mutual funds, make sure the comparisons are made using the same calculation methods and include all distributions.

THE SIZE OF A FUND

There has been some talk in the past about the effect that the size of a mutual fund has on your return.

Small funds can have a problem if you don't watch their fees. Generally, a fund needs at least $10 million under management in order to support the cost of operation. Because of that, you will see some new funds waiving costs of the fund until it reaches a certain level. To make sure you're not overpaying, just watch that the expenses remain in line with other funds. A good rule of thumb is that a fund needs about $50 million to overcome all of the operational expenses.

Smaller funds also suffer from a restriction requiring no more than 10% of assets to be in a particular stock. That doesn't give a small fund much leverage with a company because it won't be able to buy as many shares as a larger fund. On the other hand, size can work against a large fund because they have so much money to spend. If the large fund takes too great of a position in a particular stock, they may actually cause a further drop in price just because the large fund decides to sell. In addition, large funds tend to gravitate to the market mean return instead of outperforming the market. The reason for this is that you are forced to buy more and more different stocks because you have more money. At some point you are investing in most of the stocks that make up the whole market. The closer you get to this point, the more the fund's return will sharply resemble the market's return. In that case, you are probably now better off using an index fund because the cost of management and operation will be less. (For more information, see Chapter 9, "How Index Funds Can Average Your Risk.")

In the final analysis, too big of a deal is probably made regarding the size of a fund. For example, Fidelity Magellan, one of the largest funds of all times, has a track record everyone envies even though its performance is also now gravitating more to the mean. As with most analyses, fund size is just another question to raise and consider for your own satisfaction.

Portfolio Manager

Investing with a proven manager can increase your potential for success (see Chapter 6). When you select a fund, find out who the manager is and how long he or she has been with the fund. I would be concerned to discover that the manager of a fund I had selected based on its long-term track record had just left the fund and new management was in place. To offset this criticism and the inevitability of losing great managers, many funds have begun to form teams to run their funds. This prevents managers from being associated as the reason for the fund's success and when they leave the accounts go with them. The new team approach will help minimize this risk for the management company.

No matter how much the funds try to minimize it, the managers pick the fund's portfolio and some managers are better than others. Be aware of successful managers and if you see a great one moving to another fund, keep an eye on the new fund. Chances are that a successful manager at one fund will be successful at his new fund.

Dollars & Sense: Great mutual fund managers are like star athletes. There are only a few of them and they are paid well. Getting to know who the best managers are is just as important as knowing the holdings of a fund.

Evaluating Past Performance

If I've heard it once, I've heard it a hundred times from the Securities Exchange Commission (SEC), along with the National Association of Securities Dealers, (NASD): "Past performance is no guarantee of future success."

While this statement is true, past performance is a guarantee of past performance and that is important. Show me a fund that has ranked in the top ten every year for the past ten years with the same management team and I'll pick it every time over a fund in the bottom list of performance. True, the bottom performer may have a major change that causes it to leap to number one, but the odds aren't likely. While no one wants to admit that investing is a form of gambling, reality says otherwise. Every time you invest, you are putting your money on the line. Different investments have different risk/rewards (odds) and that is what makes it exciting. How you do in terms of return is dependent upon your analysis of the investment. Consequently, past performance, while not the absolute judge of the future, is an important factor nonetheless. Fortunately, in this day of high-tech information availability it is easy even for a novice to get good and inexpensive information of a fund's performance. First, you can get historical information from the fund itself. Second, you can confirm it from major financial publications such as *Money Magazine*. Remember, however, that magazines are two or three months behind because of reporting deadlines but they are excellent for annual information.

The key to looking at past performance is not to get dazzled by any one year. Any fund can be a winner in one year. It is consistency that is important. Five-year performance is a good benchmark for success and ten-year performance is even better. The other important issue when looking at performance is the economy. You cannot bury your head in the sand and simply pick the next decade's winners by the current decade's success.

The economy is a constantly changing environment. Factors that favor large companies, like low inflation and cheap interest, will dramatically affect their performance if the economy changes to higher inflation and high interest. Having picked your fund on past performance without an eye open to the future is an open invitation to disaster. In fact, by observing the economic change, you might well have turned your attention completely to the overseas market that might have a different economic environment.

Like each of the strategies we discuss, past performance is simply another tool for you to use in your analysis. Use the past performance of a fund not as an absolute, but as one of your tools that will increase the odds of successful investing in your favor.

Dollars & Sense: Investing only in each year's top-ranked fund has not proven to be a successful strategy. The reason? Changing conditions. Managers change, the markets change, the economy changes. Any one of these factors can affect future returns.

Computers, Newsletters, and Research Reports

With the growing proliferation of investors and the information age upon us, it became only natural that investors have almost as many options for investment information as actual investments.

Some of the strategies we will recommend in this book can best be applied through the speed of a computer. If computers are not your fancy, you may find that a newsletter service that does it for you is helpful. If you become an active investor, you'll find many options. In the resource section of this book, I give you my suggestions and recommendations. Part of the fun of investing is discovery. So make sure you investigate before you invest. Additionally, I'd be remiss if I didn't let you know that I also have a companion newsletter that follows the strategies in this book. The newsletter is called the *Mutual Fund Advisor* and to help you get started, I am offering a complimentary copy to all readers of this book. If you would like your copy, call my office at 1-800-333-3700 and ask for the current issue. We will send one along with our current recommendations as a thank you for buying and reading this book. You're on your way and we'll help you any way we can.

If you decide to go the high-tech route, remember, the key to financial software selection is to find one you can actually use, so try to get a demonstration first. With newsletters, hotlines and other such services, comfort and simplicity are the rule. If the strategy is too complicated, you aren't likely to stick with it. If the strategy they recommend is riskier than your tolerance, you shouldn't invest. Finally, find the program that matches the philosophy you feel is right and most comfortable. Everyone will say theirs is the best, but the proof will be how it works for you. Ask about trial subscriptions and discounts that may be available.

Let's Remember This:

- ► Learning to properly evaluate a fund can increase your return.
- ► A prospectus may be boring legalese, but it has important information.
- ► Discount broker networks offer new advantages to investors that make them a worthwhile alternative.

Table 4-3 Fidelity Funds
1-800-544-8888

Mutual Fund	Reg. $ Min.	IRA $ Min.	Load %	Investment Objective	OER %	12B-1 Fee %
Fidelity	2500	1000	0.00	Growth Income	0.64	None
FidelityAdvisor Equity Growth	2500	1000	0.00	Growth	0.84	None
Fidelity Advisor Emerging Markets Income	2500	1000	0.00	Intl. Gbl. Bond	N/A	N/A
Fidelity Advisor Equity Income	2500	1000	0.00	Equity Income	0.71	N/A
Fidelity Advisor Global Resources	2500	1000	0.00	Specialized	N/A	N/A
Fidelity Advisor Government Investment	2500	1000	0.00	Mrtg. Back US Bn.	0.75	N/A
Fidelity Advisor Growth Opportunities	2500	1000	0.00	Growth	N/A	N/A
Fidelity Advisor High-Income Municipal	2500	1000	0.00	Hi. Yld. Muni. Bond	N/A	N/A
Fidelity Advisor High-Yield	2500	1000	0.00	Hi. Yld. Crp. Bond	0.70	N/A
Fidelity Advisor Income & Growth	2500	1000	0.00	Balanced	N/A	N/A
Fidelity Advisor Intermediate Bond	2500	1000	0.00	Genl. Corp. Bond	0.61	N/A
Fidelity Advisor Intermediate Muni. Income	2500	1000	0.00	Muni. Bond	0.65	N/A
Fidelity Advisor Overseas	2500	1000	0.00	Intl. Equity	N/A	N/A

Mutual Fund	Reg. $ Min.	IRA $ Min.	Load %	Investment Objective	OER %	12B-1 Fee %
Fidelity Advisor Short Fixed-Income	2500	1000	0.00	Genl. Corp. Bond	N/A	N/A
Fidelity Advisor Short-Intermediate Muni. Income	2500	1000	0.00	Muni. Bond	N/A	N/A
Fidelity Advisor Strategic Income	2500	1000	0.00	Genl. Corp. Bond	N/A	N/A
Fidelity Advisor Strategic Opportunities	2500	1000	0.00	Growth	N/A	N/A
Fidelity Asset Manager	2500	1000	0.00	Flex Portfolio	0.97	None
Fidelity Asset Manager Growth	2500	1000	0.00	Flex Portfolio	1.15	None
Fidelity Balanced	2500	1000	0.00	Balanced	0.90	None
Fidelity Blue Chip Growth	2500	1000	3.00	Growth	1.02	None
Fidelity California Tax-Free High-Yield	2500	1000	0.00	Hi. Yld. Muni. Bnd.	0.56	None
Fidelity California Tax-Free Insured	2500	1000	0.00	CA. Muni. Bond	0.59	None
Fidelity Canada	2500	1000	3.00	Intl. Equity	1.57	None
Fidelity Capital & Income	2500	1000	0.00	Hi. Yld. Crp. Bond	0.96	None
Fidelity Capital Appreciation	2500	1000	3.00	Aggr. Growth	1.17	None
Fidelity Contra	2500	1000	3.00	Growth	1.00	None

continues

Table 4-3 Fidelity Funds (continued)
1-800-544-8888

Mutual Fund	Reg. $ Min.	IRA $ Min.	Load %	Investment Objective	OER %	12B-1 Fee %
Fidelity Convertible Securities	2500	1000	0.00	Equity Income	0.85	None
Fidelity Disciplined Equity	2500	1000	0.00	Growth	0.93	None
Fidelity Diversified International	2500	1000	3.00	Intl. Equity	1.25	None
Fidelity Dividend Growth	2500	1000	0.00	Growth	1.19	None
Fidelity Emerging Growth	2500	1000	3.00	Aggr. Growth	1.02	None
Fidelity Emerging Markets	2500	1000	3.00	Emerging Mkts.	1.52	None
Fidelity Equity Income	2500	1000	2.00	Equity Income	0.69	None
Fidelity Equity Income II	2500	1000	0.00	Equity Income	0.81	None
Fidelity Europe	2500	1000	3.00	Europe Equity	1.35	None
Fidelity Europe Capital Appreciation	2500	1000	3.00	Europe Equity	1.54	None
Fidelity Export	2500	1000	0.00	Growth	1.22	None
Fidelity Fifty	2500	1000	3.00	Aggr. Growth	1.19	None
Fidelity Global Balanced	2500	1000	0.00	Global Equity	1.33	None
Fidelity Global Bond	2500	1000	0.00	Intl. Gbl. Bond	1.14	None

Mutual Fund	Reg. $ Min.	IRA $ Min.	Load %	Investment Objective	OER %	12B-1 Fee %
Fidelity GNMA	2500	1000	0.00	Mrtg. Back US Bnd.	0.75	None
Fidelity Government Securities	2500	1000	0.00	Genl. Govt. Bond	0.69	None
Fidelity Growth & Income	2500	1000	3.00	Growth Income	0.77	None
Fidelity Growth Company	2500	1000	3.00	Growth	1.05	None
Fidelity High-Yield Tax-Free Municipal Bond	2500	1000	0.00	Hi. Yld. Muni. Bond	0.56	None
Fidelity Institutional Short-Intermediate Govt.	1000	1000	0.00	Genl. Govt. Bond	0.45	None
Fidelity Intermediate Bond	2500	1000	0.00	Hi. Qlty. Crp. Bond	0.68	None
Fidelity International Growth & Income	2500	1000	0.00	Intl. Equity	1.21	None
Fidelity Investment Grade Bond	2500	1000	0.00	Genl. Corp. Bond	0.75	None
Fidelity Japan	2500	1000	3.00	Pacific Equity	1.42	None
Fidelity Latin America	2500	1000	3.00	Intl. Equity	1.48	None
Fidelity Limited-Term Municipal Bond	2500	1000	0.00	Muni. Bond	0.56	None
Fidelity Low-Priced Stock	2500	1000	3.00	Small Company	1.11	None

continues

Table 4-3   Fidelity Funds (continued)
1-800-544-8888

Mutual Fund	Reg. $ Min.	IRA $ Min.	Load %	Investment Objective	OER %	12B-1 Fee %
Fidelity Magellan	2500	1000	3.00	Growth	0.96	None
Fidelity Massachusetts Tax-Free Municipal	2500	1000	0.00	Hi. Yld. Muni. Bond	0.54	None
Fidelity Michigan Tax-Free	2500	1000	0.00	Hi Yld. Muni. Bond	0.57	None
Fidelity Mid-Cap Stock	2500	1000	0.00	Growth	1.22	None
Fidelity Minnesota Tax-Free	2500	1000	0.00	Hi. Yld. Muni. Bond	0.59	None
Fidelity Mortgage Security	2500	1000	0.00	Mrtg. Back. US Bond	0.77	None
Fidelity Municipal Bond	2500	1000	0.00	Muni. Bond	0.53	None
Fidelity New Markets Income	2500	1000	0.00	Intl. Gbl. Bond	1.28	None
Fidelity New Millennium	2500	1000	3.00	Growth	1.29	None
Fidelity New York Tax-Free High-Yield Municipal	2500	1000	0.00	Hi. Yld. Muni. Bond	0.58	None
Fidelity Ohio Tax-Free Bond	2500	1000	0.00	Hi. Yld. Muni. Bond	0.57	None
Fidelity OTC	2500	1000	3.00	Growth	0.81	None
Fidelity Overseas	2500	1000	0.00	Intl. Equity	1.24	None

Mutual Fund	Reg. $ Min.	IRA $ Min.	Load %	Investment Objective	OER %	12B-1 Fee %
Fidelity Pacific Basin	2500	1000	3.00	Pacific Equity	1.54	None
Fidelity Puritan	2500	1000	0.00	Balanced	0.77	None
Fidelity Real Estate Investment	2500	1000	0.00	Specialized	1.03	None
Fidelity Retirement Growth	N/A	1000	0.00	Growth	1.07	None
Fidelity Select-Air Transportation	2500	1000	3.00	Specialized	2.50	None
Fidelity Select-American Gold	2500	1000	3.00	Prc. Metl. Gold	1.41	None
Fidelity Select-Automotive	2500	1000	3.00	Specialized	1.80	None
Fidelity Select-Biotechnology	2500	1000	3.00	Specialized	1.59	None
Fidelity Select-Broker/Investor Management	2500	1000	3.00	Specialized	2.54	None
Fidelity Select-Chemicals	2500	1000	3.00	Specialized	1.51	None
Fidelity Select-Computers	2500	1000	3.00	Specialized	1.69	None
Fidelity Select-Construction & Housing	2500	1000	3.00	Specialized	1.74	None
Fidelity Select-Consumer Products	2500	1000	3.00	Specialized	2.49	None
Fidelity Select-Defense & Aerospace	2500	1000	3.00	Specialized	2.49	None
Fidelity Select-Developing Communication	2500	1000	3.00	Specialized	1.56	None

continues

Table 4-3   Fidelity Funds (continued)
1-800-544-8888

Mutual Fund	Reg. $ Min.	IRA $ Min.	Load %	Investment Objective	OER %	12B-1 Fee %
Fidelity Select-Electronics	2500	1000	3.00	Specialized	1.71	None
Fidelity Select-Energy	2500	1000	3.00	Specialized	1.85	None
Fidelity Select-Energy Services	2500	1000	3.00	Specialized	1.79	None
Fidelity Select-Environmental Services	2500	1000	3.00	Specialized	2.01	None
Fidelity Select-Financial Services	2500	1000	3.00	Specialized	1.54	None
Fidelity Select-Food Agriculture	2500	1000	3.00	Specialized	1.68	None
Fidelity Select-Health Care	2500	1000	3.00	Specialized	1.36	None
Fidelity Select-Home Finance	2500	1000	3.00	Specialized	1.45	None
Fidelity Select-Industrial Equipment	2500	1000	3.00	Specialized	1.78	None
Fidelity Select-Industrial Materials	2500	1000	3.00	Specialized	1.53	None
Fidelity Select-Insurance	2500	1000	3.00	Specialized	2.34	None
Fidelity Select-Leisure & Entertainment	2500	1000	3.00	Specialized	1.62	None
Fidelity Select-Medical Delivery	2500	1000	3.00	Specialized	1.45	None
Fidelity Select-Multimedia	2500	1000	3.00	Specialized	2.03	None

Mutual Fund	Reg. $ Min.	IRA $ Min.	Load %	Investment Objective	OER %	12B-1 Fee %
Fidelity Select-Natural Gas	2500	1000	3.00	Specialized	1.66	None
Fidelity Select-Paper & Forest Products	2500	1000	3.00	Specialized	1.87	None
Fidelity Select-Precious Metals & Minerals	2500	1000	3.00	Prc. Metl. Gold	1.46	None
Fidelity Select-Regional Banks	2500	1000	3.00	Specialized	1.56	None
Fidelity Select-Retailing	2500	1000	3.00	Specialized	1.96	None
Fidelity Select-Software/Computer Services	2500	1000	3.00	Specialized	1.50	None
Fidelity Select-Technology	2500	1000	3.00	Specialized	1.56	None
Fidelity Select-Telecommunications	2500	1000	3.00	Specialized	1.55	None
Fidelity Select-Transportation	2500	1000	3.00	Specialized	2.36	None
Fidelity Select-Utilities Growth	2500	1000	3.00	Specialized	1.42	None
Fidelity Short-Term Bond	2500	1000	0.00	Genl. Corp. Bond	0.69	None
Fidelity Short-Term World Income	2500	1000	0.00	Intl. Gbl. Bond	1.01	None
Fidelity Small-Cap Stock	2500	1000	3.00	Small Company	0.90	None
Fidelity Southeast Asia	2500	1000	3.00	Pacific Equity	1.47	None
Fidelity Stock Selector	2500	1000	0.00	Growth	1.09	None

continues

Table 4-3   Fidelity Funds (continued)
1-800-544-8888

Mutual Fund	Reg. $ Min.	IRA $ Min.	Load %	Investment Objective	OER %	12B-1 Fee %
Fidelity Trend	2500	1000	0.00	Growth	0.89	None
Fidelity U.S. Equity Index	100,000	1000	0.00	Growth Income	0.28	None
Fidelity Utilities	2500	1000	0.00	Specialized	0.87	None
Fidelity Value	2500	1000	0.00	Growth	1.08	None
Fidelity Worldwide	2500	1000	3.00	Global Equity	1.32	None

▼

HOW TO PICK THE BEST MONEY MARKET FUND

WHAT WE ARE GOING TO TALK ABOUT IN THIS CHAPTER:

- ▶ The Avantages and Disadvantages of Money Market Accounts
- ▶ How to Pick the Best Money Market Fund
- ▶ Comparing Discount Broker Money Market Accounts

It wasn't that long ago that mutual fund money markets were unheard of for most of the public. In the early '80s, I was doing investment seminars across the country and just the concept of using a place other than the town bank for checking and savings brought questions of doubt and concern from the audience. During those years, I was only able to interest people in mutual fund money markets because the yield was so much better. It was common for banks to be paying 2%–3% lower on their accounts compared to mutual fund money markets. Naturally, as fund money markets caught on, and the banks' negative flow of cash moved out of their vaults and into mutual funds, the banks became more competitive with their rates. You can still get better rates on mutual fund money markets, but not by much, and there are still advantages to having local lender relations that may outweigh the slight increase in return.

In the past two years we have also seen banking regulations change to allow all banks to compete and have their own mutual fund accounts. This will now give banks the opportunity to tie their own money market funds and equity funds into a master account like the big mutual fund families have done. The result is the banking industry's attempt to make itself the one-stop shop for all of your financial needs. While this change will bring added convenience, it will also bring new conflicts of interest that the banking industry has overlooked or at least closed its eyes to. Will the banks and their commission-oriented brokers recommend the bank's mutual funds to very conservative investors who have been traditional CD buyers? Will loans be offered on more favorable terms to the bank's mutual fund buyers? The answers to these and other ethical questions are unanswered at this point, but some of the early complaints hint that there may be problems ahead.

What Do Money Market Funds Do With Your Money?

From an investment standpoint, money market mutual funds do the same thing that banks do with your money. They buy short-term debt instruments. Because they have large amounts of cash, they can buy large blocks of paper that you as an individual would be unable to buy and they can make a spread on the transaction which becomes their profit.

For example, you can go to your bank and buy a CD from them. In doing so, you are loaning them money for a set rate of interest. A money fund manager can also go to the bank and loan them money by buying large CDs, referred to as jumbo CDs. Again, because of their size, they can demand a higher interest than an individual can get. The money market will pay you your pro-rata portion of the earnings and keep a management fee and expenses out of the spread between what they pay you and what they earn. Although the spreads are small, the amount of money moving is so large that banks can become very profitable just playing the spread.

The disadvantage of mutual fund money markets compared to bank money markets is that mutual funds do not have Federal Deposit Insurance (FDIC insurance). The insurance offers bank depositors protection on the first $100,000 they have in an account in their name. From a practical standpoint, the risk of loss from a mutual fund not redeeming your investment is extremely low. If you are concerned, then you can restrict yourself from dealing with anything but the largest mutual fund companies, but I wouldn't even worry about that.

WHY USE MUTUAL FUND MONEY MARKETS?

I like mutual fund money markets because of their earnings and their convenience. If you select your money market fund at the same mutual fund company that you invest in, then you can open what is most often referred to as a cash management account (CMA). The CMA accounts are a master account for all your financial needs. You can also get similar accounts with your broker and some banks have finally started competing, but I still think the mutual funds have a better program over the banks.

Money Talks: Cash management account is the generic term for the service that provides a master account linking all of your financial activities together. The mutual fund families all have their own name for the account. An example of one such service is the Fidelity Ultra Account sponsored by Fidelity Investments. The account will show your monthly activity for checking, debit card, money market accounts, mutual funds, and stock purchases.

The CMA account ties all of your investments with that fund together with the money market account. The CMA generally offers you check-writing privileges and even a debit card that you can use like your credit card to access ATMs or purchase goods and services. As you use the card, the money is automatically taken out of your account. So, unlike a credit card, you do have to have the money in your account before making a purchase.

Some CMA accounts also offer bill paying services or monthly withdrawal programs if you are on a fixed income. At the end of the month you get one statement showing all of your checking, debit card, and investment activity. This is a nice service if you are a lousy recordkeeper.

The biggest advantage the mutual fund money markets offer is that the account can be used as a neutral home when the market dictates that you should move out of stock or bond funds. Additionally, because the accounts are connected, you can have an easy automatic savings program sweeping a certain portion of your money out of your money market and into your stock fund on a periodic basis.

Dollars & Sense: Use cash management accounts like a jumbo savings account, running all of your credit card, checking, and mutual fund purchases through the same account. This will simplify your year-end tax accounting tremendously.

How Do You Select the Best Money Market?

The four criteria you should use to select your money market account are:

1. Yield. How much interest will this account pay you?

2. Expenses. How much are you being charged for this service?

3. Services. What do they offer?

4. Fund Returns. Is the performance of the other funds in this family (stocks and bonds) up to your standards? Because overall yield is your major consideration, you would not want to put your money market account with a fund company that otherwise had poor returns, unless that was all the business you planned to do with the fund. Remember, your net overall return from all your investments with that fund family is more important than just the return on your money market account.

    The exception to this would be if you had adequate liquid dollars that allowed you to have a second money market fund based primarily on yield or special circumstances, such as tax-free or foreign money markets.

What About Brokerage Money Market Accounts?

Stock brokerage firms also offer money market funds and even their own CMA accounts. The only problem with them is that you are immediately put on a broker's call list to buy the firm's investments. Unless you absolutely can't resist working with a full service broker, I would refer you to a discount brokerage firm like Charles Schwab & Co., Fidelity's Brokerage Service, or Jack White Securities. These companies have excellent CMA accounts and allow you to connect them to their large, no-load mutual fund trading markets. Using this approach is like having your CMA account connected to many of the major fund families at the same time.

Table 5-1 Cash Management Accounts
Discount Brokers

Company	Min. Initial Deposit	Fees	Current Interest 6/96
Charles Schwab & Co. (SchwabOne Acct.) 1-800-435-4000	$5,000	No annual fee. No monthly fee unless balance of account (cash plus securities) falls below $5,000 mark. At that point, face $5 monthly fee. Unlimited check writing. Debit card available.	4.508%
Fidelity Disc. Brokerage (Ultra Service Account) 1-800-544-9797	$10,000	Annual fee of $30. Face $12 monthly fee if balance of account (cash plus securities) falls below $2,500. Unlimited check writing. Debit card available.	4.45%
Jack White & Co. 1-800-233-3411	$10,000	No annual fee. No monthly fee unless balance of account (cash plus securities) falls below $500. At that point, face $2 monthly fee. Unlimited check writing. Debit card available.	4.51%

continues

Table 5-1 Cash Management Accounts (continued)
Discount Brokers

Company	Min. Initial Deposit	Fees	Current Interest 6/96
Fidelity Spartan Brokerage Account 1-800-544-9797	$20,000	$30 annual fee is waived if you do the required trading. This is strictly a trading account. You can only purchase stocks and options in this account—no mutual funds. Must be a proved trader to open this type of account (40+ trades per year). No checks or debit card available.	3.942%

LET'S REMEMBER THIS:

▶ Money markets are a safe place to park your money between investments.

▶ Not all money markets are the same and knowing the difference can increase your return.

▶ Cash management accounts offer a low cost accounting and banking service for investors.

How to Pick the Best Stock Mutual Fund

What We Are Going to Talk About in This Chapter:

- ▶ The Five Steps to Buying a Successful Mutual Fund
- ▶ The Three Components of a Good Fund
- ▶ Top Growth Funds that Pass Our Test

With over 3,500 stock mutual funds currently available in the marketplace, it is no wonder that there is confusion on the part of an investor when it comes time to actually pick which one they should invest in. To compound the confusion, stock funds are broken down into numerous categories including aggressive growth, growth, growth and income, and specialized funds. Consequently, in order to avoid a simple random selection approach, a specific plan of attack must be designed to increase the opportunity for success.

In an earlier section of this book, I stated that an investor should review his financial goals before making the decision to invest. If you are investing in stock mutual funds, then I hope you have made the conscious decision to do so because of the particular goals you have laid out for yourself. Specifically, among the goals that I would expect to see is the desire to obtain maximum growth potential for your invested dollars.

If you have selected higher current income with some risk, then I would expect you to be considering equity/income or growth/income type mutual funds. Whatever funds you are selecting, I want it to match up to your goals and objectives on your financial profile.

Dollars & Sense:

Five steps before you buy stock mutual funds:

1. Know your goals;

2. Know your needs;

3. Know your risk tolerance;

4. Research and analyze the funds; and

5. Monitor your selections.

WHAT TYPE OF RETURN CAN YOU REALISTICALLY EXPECT TO MAKE?

Forgetting all the hype associated with the promotion of mutual funds, it is important that we look at the type of return that an individual can reasonably expect to make. There are many ways that you could come up with this projection, but I think it is only fair that we look at the fund's past accomplishments. The difficulty with reviewing past performance is that you are also dealing with past historical circumstances. For example, carving out the period from 1970 to 1975 and analyzing the return of the stock mutual funds would require that you be subject to the very dismal performance of the stock market during a substantial period of that time. Another view would be to take a historical representation since the beginning of time and averaging your return. This certainly has some degree of merit because you are considering all different types of economies and external conditions. Even so, this type of analysis has its own flaws because it may persuade you from acting in the exact manner you should because the circumstances have slightly altered.

Having made this caveat regarding any study of historical performances, I believe it is nevertheless important to look at such a chart. Referring to Figure 6-1, you will see a chart that depicts both the annualized average return of the Standard & Poors

Figure 6-1   Growth of $10,000 Investment

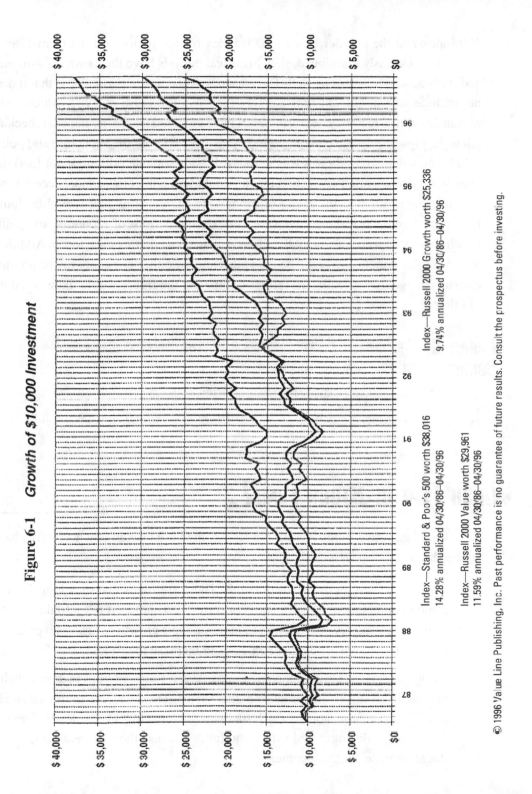

Index—Standard & Poor's 500 worth $38,016
14.28% annualized 04/30/86–04/30/96

Index—Russell 2000 Value worth $29,961
11.59% annualized 04/30/86–04/30/96

Index—Russell 2000 Growth worth $25,336
9.74% annualized 04/30/86–04/30/96

500 Index and the broader Russell 2000 Index for the period of time from 1986 to 1996. As previously mentioned, such historical periods have their own built-in bias, and this one certainly has as well. The reason for this bias in particular is that it does not include any significant bear market other than the crash of 1987, which had a reasonably quick recovery. Nevertheless, I have included this particular chart because it has the closest relevance to our period of history and both the economic and political climates that we find ourselves in today. It is reasonable (although not fact) that even with a new market correction that no doubt will come, these more recent types of returns are closer to the realm of probability than returns that would be found further back in historical time but were made during periods of economic and political climates that were substantially different than those that we face today. Additionally, a similar conclusion could be made that should either our economy or political climate change dramatically, the returns outlined in the figure would likewise be out of kilter.

Dollars & Sense: The three critical steps to selecting a mutual fund investment include:

1. Historical performance;

2. Internal makeup of the fund selected; and

3. The current trend of the market in general and the specific fund under analysis.

Which Type of Stock Fund?

Out of all the mutual funds that deal in stocks, they are broken down into five basic subheadings.

1. Growth and Aggressive Growth Funds. These are funds that seek long-term capital appreciation as their major concern. The funds that fall into the aggressive category will attempt to increase their growth by using leverage, margining, options, and other strategies to increase their yield.

2. Equity Income or Growth/Income Funds. These funds attempt to derive their income from stocks that produce higher yields. These include preferred stocks as well as common stocks, which traditionally have higher dividends. These funds can be distinguished from bond funds because they concentrate on stocks to generate the income.

3. Value Funds. These are funds that concentrate on strong fundamentals in the underlying stocks, seeking those which have below price-earnings ratios believing that these will produce superior yields in the long term.

4. Sector Funds. These are mutual funds that specialize in a particular industry. (See Chapter 12 for more information.)

5. Specialized Funds. These funds deal in global or international stocks, small companies, or any other degree of specialization.

Money Talks: The term "value," as used with value funds, can be misleading. Most fund managers think of a stock held in a value fund as having value because its price has under-performed compared to the intrinsic worth of the stock. Consequently, the stocks in a value fund may be unknown. This definition is frequently different for many investors, who think of a value stock as being fully valued like some blue chip stocks.

Each of these sub-categories have their own personal advantages and disadvantages and I have attempted to go into some of the more extensive categories in detail in other chapters. However, when attempting to select the particular stock fund that you want to invest in, you must understand the categories and make sure you have matched them to your financial goals.

In order to help you determine which funds meet your needs, I think it is important to once again review past performance as a launching point to study the funds. Figure 6-2 shows the returns of the five categories of the period of time from 1986 to 1996. As I have cautioned before, do not use these past performances as a mark of what you will receive in the future but only as a judge and an understanding of how these funds have performed relative to each other during a historical period of time that had a strong uptrend in the market.

Once you understand the type of funds that are available and the historical performance of these funds in similar market conditions, the next step is to select the category and look at the individual funds within that category. Once again, I would use past performance of the funds as a starting point, utilizing at least a ten-year track record as an initial threshold. Some people feel that the ten-year requirement eliminates some of the recent funds that have developed and are good performers and there is no question that criticism is valid. However, by using a ten-year track record as an initial threshold, you do start off with funds that have at least proven themselves over time.

Figure 6-2 *Growth of $10,000 Investment*

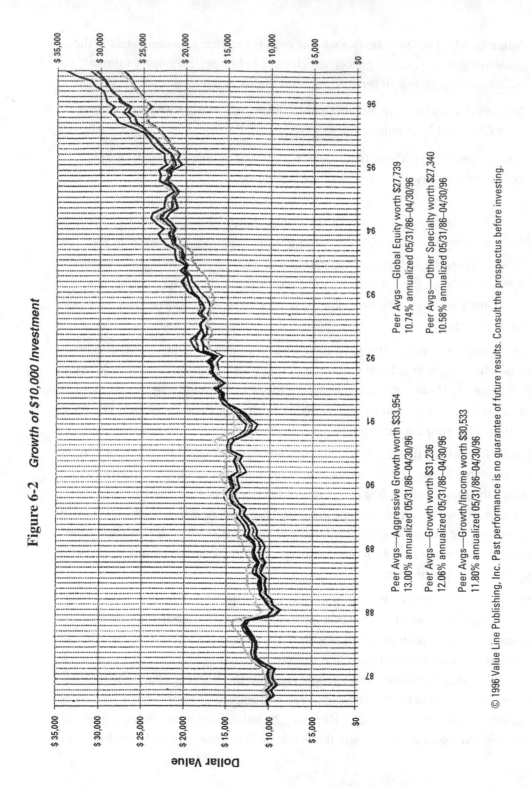

Peer Avgs—Aggressive Growth worth $33,954
13.00% annualized 05/31/86–04/30/96

Peer Avgs—Growth worth $31,236
12.06% annualized 05/31/86–04/30/96

Peer Avgs—Growth/Income worth $30,533
11.80% annualized 05/31/86–04/30/96

Peer Avgs—Global Equity worth $27,739
10.74% annualized 05/31/86–04/30/96

Peer Avgs—Other Specialty worth $27,340
10.58% annualized 05/31/86–04/30/96

© 1996 Value Line Publishing, Inc. Past performance is no guarantee of future results. Consult the prospectus before investing.

Dollars & Sense: While past performance is never a guarantee of future success, it does tell you a lot about what the fund has done in various market environments and provides information to help you understand what it might do in the present environment.

After you have selected a group of funds from this first filtering process, the next thing I would do is take this narrowed group and run it through two more inspection filters. One would be a five-year return filter, and the second would be a one-year return filter. This means that I would simply narrow the list of my ten-year performers by those funds that had also performed well during the last five years, and then narrow it further by those who had performed well during the previous one year. By using this filtration process, you are starting with funds that have historically performed well and then confirming that their tendency to perform well has continued over more recent periods of time.

After you have narrowed down this list by using the filtration process, it should be narrowed even further by looking at current performance. This can be narrowed down by examining performance as recently as the past 30 days. But I believe it is more important for you to use a view between three and six months in order to delete potential variations that have occurred accidentally. (See Chapter 11, "The Profitline Strategy," for more information on how to do this.)

The previous process of reviewing a historical return can easily be done by use of the computer and various programs that are available in the public marketplace. However, for those who may not be computer literate or do not have access to the software required, a slightly more time-consuming process would be to refer to magazines that annually perform calculations similar to the ones I have just outlined. The best magazines for this purpose are *Money Magazine, Business Week, Kiplinger's,* or *Forbes.* Each of these publications annually produce an analysis similar to the ones I have just mentioned and the most recent edition would be available at your local library if you don't have a copy of your own. Additionally, you can write to these various magazines who frequently allow consumers to buy that particular edition for a relatively small charge.

While the process I have just described is the best and I think safest way to pick a fund, it does have one negative. It eliminates the new fast growth fund. As a general rule, I don't recommend new funds. There are, as always, exceptions. The first exception deals with a proven manager who breaks away from a mutual fund to start his own. The most recent example of this was Garrett Van Wagoner who left Govett after setting record-breaking years in 1993 and 1994. The performance in 1994 was especially good since it was generally considered an off year. To eliminate using this talented manager simply because he won't have a five-year track record would be a mistake.

The second exception involves the creation of "clone" funds by an already established fund. A clone fund is formed when a mutual fund company believes that a certain fund has grown too large to accomplish its plan. When this occurs, the fund closes to new investors. Rather than lose potential investors to a competitor, the investment company forms another fund identical to the successful one. This new fund is the clone. The reason the new fund works is because the company believes a fund that is too large will keep the manager from narrowing his selection A manager can never have more than 5% of the dollars of the fund committed to any one company. Therefore, a manager must find more good companies when more dollars are coming into the fund. This is a job that becomes more difficult almost by definition. A fairly recent example of this was with the mutual fund "Windsor" and "Windsor II," its clone. Because the clone was established to model the successful moves of the main fund, there is no reason for it not to perform well if it has the same management team.

MAKEUP OF THE INDIVIDUAL FUND

By now you have narrowed down your stock mutual fund selection to a more manageable group. Narrowing it down further requires you to order a prospectus on the fund and actually review its internal makeup. I will tell you that most people have never gone to the trouble of making this sort of inspection, but I will also suggest that those investors would be surprised about what they had actually invested in if they had taken the time to do so. Consequently, I will point out to you the areas of the prospectus that I think you should look at in order to narrow down your selection.

Dollars & Sense: Use clone funds to take advantage of successful funds that are now closed to new buyers. Make sure the manager is the same and that the objectives are still the same. This information can be found in the prospectus or by calling the service representative.

The following five points should be utilized in reviewing a stock fund before making a final selection:

1. The portfolio manager's time with the fund.

2. The age of the fund.

3. The cost of the fund.

4. The size of the fund.

5. Portfolio makeup.

1. **Portfolio Manager.** The portfolio manager of a stock mutual fund is extremely important because he is the person that is picking the stocks that will be held in the fund. In the past year, several of the major funds have attempted to reduce the importance that investors place on the manager by shifting the managers between various mutual funds. They have attempted to minimize this change with what I refer to as "fund speak" and making other excuses for this move. In reality, what they have attempted to do is make sure that individual managers are no longer tied closely with the fund. This is because in recent years some of the managers, such as Fidelity's Peter Lynch, have become so well-known that people begin to invest with the manager as opposed to the mutual fund company. This is fine as long as the manager remains with the fund, but if the manager decides to launch off on his own, the mutual fund investment company could very well find that they are left holding the bag when all of the millions of dollars that the investors have put with this particular manager leave with the manager.

Additionally, in order to minimize the manager's prestige, the funds have also attempted to match managers together in a team approach. Again, while they will say that this is being done in order to help the funds, in reality the reason is to minimize the importance of the manager. I have referred to this dissemination of bad information as "fund speak" because it is a typical situation where the funds do not necessarily give you the whole truth for their actions. A manager is the single most important individual related to your investment and his past background, including historical record, is extremely important. Consequently, if you can find managers who have a long-term track record and they are still with one of the funds that you are investigating as a potential investment, I would consider this extremely positive. If, on the other hand, you find that the fund has an entirely new manager and no track record with either the existing fund or another similar fund, then I would consider this a negative because you have no idea as to how this performance has been nor what to expect in the future.

2. Age of the Fund. As previously mentioned, I don't like new funds as a general rule. However, by eliminating a new fund from your selection, you may very well be missing out on a golden opportunity. Nevertheless, you should place great emphasis on how funds have performed. Although the regulators tell you that past performance is no guarantee of future success, it does, nevertheless, show you what has happened in the past and that is important even if not a predictor of the future. I believe that a good rule of thumb would be for a fund to have at least a five-year track record before you make it one of your investment choices. If that eliminates one of your funds from possible selection, so be it. You may lose out on a potential winner every now and then because of this process, but it is a good exercise of prudence. At the beginning of the chapter I mentioned two exceptions to the rule. A third exception that could be made would be for index funds, which are based on a specific category that has been in existence for years. An example of this would be if one of the mutual fund companies began a new index fund centered around all of the companies that currently make up the Standard & Poor's 500. The fact that this was a new fund would not concern me because the mode of operation that it is following has been in existence for some time and what they are buying has no variable.

3. Cost of Ownership. I think cost of ownership of the fund is important but it should only be used as one of the weighted factors. For example, if one of the funds that you are analyzing had a consistent ten-year track record 4% or 5% better than another fund whose cost of ownership was slightly lower on an annual basis, then I would certainly lean toward the fund with the better track record rather than the one that had lower cost of ownership. This being said, the cost of ownership certainly is important for two funds similar in nature. If a fund produces a yield of 12% a year but its cost of ownership is 1% as opposed to a similar fund whose cost of ownership is 2%, it certainly changes the net yield to you. There are four things to be viewed in terms of the cost of ownership:

    ▶   Initial sales charges

    ▶   12-B-1 marketing expenses

- ► Operating expenses
- ► Class of shares

The up-front sales commission is typically referred to as the load of the fund. I have previously indicated to you that there has been no statistical data which shows that a loaded fund is better than a no-load fund. Consequently, given a choice between two funds, one of which has an up-front load and one that has no load, an investor is better off with the no-load fund.

12-B-1 fees are another way for a fund to generate or pay a load to marketing salesman without taking the load up front. In this particular case, the mutual fund company would advance the fee or commission to the salesman, and then by charging you a 12-B-1 fee over your course of ownership, they would be reimbursed for having advanced this fee to the salesman who sold the product. In short, these fees are just another form of commission and should be avoided.

The operating expenses of the fund are fairly straightforward in that they are the cost that the management company running the fund charges for its services. There is some variation in this number and it is simply a comparison between individual companies.

The class of fund that you are purchasing is one of the most misunderstood concepts in mutual fund investing. Not all mutual fund stock is offered in the same way to all investors. Funds frequently have two classes of units, and sometimes three or four. The difference between the classes of units that the fund offers is in the fees taken out of the classes. For example, class A units in a particular mutual fund may have no 12-B-1 fees. On the other hand, class B units of the same fund may charge 12-B-1 fees. Depending on how you are buying this mutual fund, either direct from the fund itself or through a salesman, you would be offered one of the different classes of the fund. It is clear in looking at this example that unless you understand these classes, you would be paying more simply by being issued the class B units. I have a strong objection to mutual fund classes, but they are here to stay. In fact, we are likely to see them more often throughout the industry.

4. Size of the Fund. A great deal of emphasis used to be placed upon the size of a particular fund. I have mentioned to you that people were cautioned about investing into too small of a fund simply because the cost of administration added an additional burden and expense. On the other hand, large funds were

a concern simply because after awhile, depending on size, they became unwieldy and tended to gravitate to the market average. The most extreme example of size is the Fidelity Magellan which now has over $50 billion under management. Because of its size, it must purchase such a large number of different companies that it is starting to act more like an index fund. Therefore, its performance is starting to move toward the mean returns. Although over the years its overall performance has been great, time will tell if its size is now becoming a burden. The bottom line as it relates to the size of the fund is that, in general, I think it makes very little difference. I'm much more concerned about the other factors.

5. Portfolio Makeup. The final point regarding the characteristics of the fund itself is to look at the actual makeup of the stock in its portfolio. What type of companies does it hold? Are the companies blue chip or small cap companies? In your initial investigation of a mutual fund, you may not know the difference between these categories. However, ultimately your understanding of the stocks that make up your mutual fund is as important as your understanding of its past performance. The reason is because the current portfolio is the single determinate of how this mutual fund will succeed in the near term as opposed of the past term. In looking at the portfolio, you might also pay attention to the turnover of that portfolio by the manager. If the portfolio is experiencing a low turnover, that would tell you that the manager currently has a long-term view of the market. Additionally, low turnover assists your fund by decreasing cost of sales when the manager buys and sells stocks within the portfolio. Additionally, a lower turnover reduces capital gains taxes that are ultimately passed on to you as an investor on an annual basis.

Two Quick Comparative Tests

A fund's Beta ratio is also an important yardstick to look at regarding the fund that you are analyzing. The Beta indicates the firm's past price volatility relative to a certain stock market index. The closer the Beta ranking is to 1.00, the closer its volatility to the average of the market that it is indexing. This measuring gauge is one of the single best determinations that you can use to narrow the selection of a fund based on your conservative or aggressive tendencies. (See Chapter 8 for additional information.)

A second statistic that is rarely discussed is a fund's percentile R-squared. This term explains the relationship between the mutual fund's individual return and a particular market index such as the S&P 500.

Most equity funds have an R-squared between 80% and 90%, which means that a large portion of that fund's total return is determined by the actual performance of the overall market as opposed to anything that the fund itself is doing. The closer the percentage gets to 100%, the closer the fund is performing in line with the market. For example, an index fund would have an R-squared ranking of 100%. If you were looking at a fund that had an R-squared percentile close to 100% but you were paying additional loads or fees to participate, it is likely that you would be better off investing in an index fund because the fund you are analyzing is really a disguised index fund. On the other hand, a fund whose R-squared was below the 80% mark would tend to show you that its performance was less predictive simply on the performance of the overall market. Consequently, if it had the low R-squared ranking and yet was a top performing fund, it would tend to tell you that the managers were doing a superb job.

The Final Analysis

After you have done your historical research, made your selections and reviewed the individual fund's internal makeup, I would apply the Profitline Strategy to this final selection. (See Chapter 11 for further information.)

In order to make your final cut, the fund must be above its 39-week moving average and trending up. That means that the current price movements overall trend must be positive. The stronger its current positive momentum, the better. If the fund's relative strength is stronger than the general market and stronger than other funds in its peer group, you have a good fund.

Once you have made your fund selections and invested, then you have two major alternatives. Do you follow the buy and hold camp or do you follow the Profitline Strategy? My recommendation is to use the Profitline Strategy. Use your short-term moving average as a warning signal and use the long-term average as your sell signal.

In the meantime, as long as your fund stays above the moving averages, then you should stay invested and even add to your position.

Closing Remarks on Fund Picks

I have just taken you through a complete process of picking the best mutual fund. Very few people other than the professionals go through this type of selection process, but if you do then you will increase your returns. Naturally, no system is perfect, just like we make mistakes in our own life. Yet we all know that through education and work we can improve our chance of success. The same is true for mutual fund investing. There is no good substitute for the knowledgeable hard-working investor.

Ten Growth Funds That Pass the Test

The following funds have been selected to give you examples of ten funds that pass the tests offered in this chapter. Before you invest in any of them, make sure they also pass the current trend test outlined in Chapter 11, "The Profitline Strategy."

Table 6-1

Fund Name & Phone No.	Inception Date	Managers Tenure	Expense Ratio %	Assets (Mil $)	5 Yr. Return
Brandywine Fund (800) 338-1579	12/12/85	10.5 Years	1.08%	4,210	21.02
Columbia Growth (800) 547-1707	08/31/67	4.5 Years	.76%	848	15.59
INVESCO Dynamics (800) 525-8085	02/17/67	3.5 Years	1.16%	624	20.11
Janus Twenty (800) 525-8983	04/26/85	8 Years	1.00%	3,057	15.03
PBHG Growth (800) 433-0051	12/19/85	11 Years	1.50%	3,572	31.95
Scudder Development (800) 225-2470	01/18/71	8 Years	1.23%	877	18.66

Fund Name & Phone No.	Inception Date	Managers Tenure	Expense Ratio %	Assets (Mil $)	5 Yr. Return
SteinRoc Capital Opportunities (800) 338-2550	03/31/69	7 Years	1.05%	332	26.50
Strong Opportunity (800) 368-1030	12/31/85	11 Years	1.30%	1,327	17.29
T. Rowe Price New Horizons (800) 638-5660	01/01/60	9 Years	.90%	3,137	23.10
Vanguard PRIMECAP (800) 662-7447	11/30/84	12 Years	.58%	3,236	17.60

LET'S REMEMBER THIS:

▶ Studying a mutual funds past performance doesn't guarantee success, but it does help you understand how a fund has performed under various economic circumstances.

▶ Consistent and successful management is an excellent indicator of a funds success.

▶ Cost of ownership can make a big difference in your return. Watch out for initial fees, high management and operating expenses, and redemption fees as warnings.

▼

How to Pick the Best Bond Fund

What We Are Going to Talk About in This Chapter:

- ▶ The Different Types of Bond Funds
- ▶ How to Determine the Risk of a Bond Fund
- ▶ Why Bond Funds May Have a Place in Your Portfolio

The first impression most people have when deciding on the selection of a bond fund is that they are all basically the same. The investor is looking for income on his investment and the first thought is to simply compare yields and make the selection. The second thought that people have when considering the selection of a bond fund is that it is a safe investment. The reality of these thoughts is that both are, in fact, false.

In the first instance, bond funds are certainly not all the same. In fact, surprisingly to many people, there are more categories of bond funds than there are equity funds. Bond funds are first broken down into three categories just based on their maturity levels: short-term, intermediate, and long-term bonds. Next, bonds can be broken down into eight specific areas to invest in: U.S. government securities, mortgage-backed instruments, investment grade corporate bonds, medium grade corporates, high yield or junk bonds, investment grade municipal (tax-free), high yield municipal (tax-free), and global. The result of these various category offerings is that there are 24 possible combinations. This is not to say that the mutual funds treat them as individual categories and do not blend them together, because the opposite is true. The fund managers frequently use the various advantages and disadvantages of each possibility to make adjustments in the overall yield of a particular portfolio.

The second issue that has confused investors is the risk associated with bonds. For years, a bond investment was considered highly stable with very little volatility. If you invested in a high corporate bond paying a 7% yield, chances are that even if you had to sell the bond before maturity there would have been very little fluctuation in value.

The stability factor for bonds has changed since the early '80s due to the strong fluctuations that we now see in interest rates. The reason is because the value of the principal amount of a bond is directly related to interest rates. As interest rates go up in value, the principal of underlying bonds decreases in amount. The opposite is equally as true; as interest rates fall, the value of the principal underlying the bond increases in value. In some ways, individual bonds are better suited to take out the variability in the price fluctuation. This is because with an individual bond, if the price fluctuates dramatically, an investor can simply hold the bond until maturity. Ultimately you will receive your principal and the yield promised when the bond was purchased. This is assuming there is no default of the bond. Mutual funds, on the other hand, fluctuate tremendously in value with volatility in interest rates. Because there is turnover of the bonds held within the mutual fund itself, as an investor you will be receiving your pro-rata portion of capital gains and/or losses during your holding period. Additionally, there is no assurance that by maintaining the mutual fund it will return to its original value because the portfolio of bonds is constantly being turned.

In addition to interest rate risks, we have also seen the recent introduction of the use of derivatives in bond portfolios. Derivatives are simply new instruments or securities derived from commonly known instruments. A good example of a derivative would be the use of zero-coupon treasury bonds as an ownership vehicle instead of owning the underlying treasury security. The advantage or disadvantage of a derivative is that they tend to increase the risk/reward ratio. For example, if you own a bond and its interest coupon has a duration of 12 years, the price of the bond will rise or fall approximately 12% for every 1% change in the interest rate. On the other hand, if you owned a thirty-year zero-coupon bond with a duration of 30 years, the principal value changes 30% with each 1% change in interest rates. As you can see, that is a dramatic change in the risk and the reasons that bonds are no longer considered conservative.

Dollars & Sense: Contrary to the media hype, derivatives are not all bad. The recent problem with derivatives was that investors didn't understand what it was or more particularly, what it was derived from. Consequently, some investors were putting their money in more volatile securities than they thought. If you understand the derivative and what it is, you may consciously find they have a place in your portfolio. As always, the key is understanding.

What to Look For in a Bond Fund

As a general rule of thumb, you want to make sure that the fund has at least $25 or $30 million to make sure its in a size range to cover its expenses. Another way to view the expense situation is simply to do an analysis to determine what the actual cost of the fund is per dollar invested. As mentioned in the analysis of equity funds, a new bond fund may very well waive some of its early start-up costs in order to make sure it is competitive with the other market.

The age of a bond fund is also not as important to me as the age of an equity fund. Nevertheless, I have a built-in bias for new funds for the simple reason that new ideas frequently mean unproven ideas, and unproven ideas add a degree of risk that you as an investor may not be willing to take. Consequently, because the number of funds available with good investment companies is numerous, there is no real reason not to stick with those that have proven track records.

Some people feel that the portfolio manager is not as important in a bond fund as they are in equity funds. This may be true on some relative scale, however, the manager is nevertheless a very important individual. There are some people who are suitable to the management of bond portfolios, and there are others who are more suitable to the gyrations of an equity portfolio. Consequently, you want to have your bond fund managed by a seasoned veteran in the bond industry.

The cost of operating the bond fund is an important consideration. In fact, when you are talking about bond funds and looking to obtain certain yields, the cost and expense ratios become extremely important because they take away from your yield.

The overall return of a fund that has the same credit quality and maturity will be dramatically effected by things such as commissions, marketing expenses, and operating costs.

Dollars & Sense:

Five key features for bond fund selection:

1. Cost, including on-going expense;
2. Management expertise;
3. Age of fund;
4. Type compared to your needs; and
5. Quality

How Do You Determine the Credit Quality of Your Portfolio?

Fortunately for investors, bonds are rated by major rating services that have been around for years and have proven their knowledge and ability. The major services all use a series of letters of the alphabet to designate the higher-ranking bonds based on higher combinations of letters. For a comparison of the top services and their rankings, please refer to Table 7-1.

Table 7-1   Bond Rating Services

Bank Grade (investment grade) Bonds		
STANDARD & POOR'S	**MOODY'S**	**INTERPRETATION**
AAA	Aaa	Highest rating. Capacity to repay principal & interest judged high.
AA	Aa	Very strong. Only slightly less secure than the highest rating.
A	A	Felt to be slightly more susceptible to bad economic conditions.

Speculative (non-investment grade) Bonds		
STANDARD & POOR'S	**MOODY'S**	**INTERPRETATION**
BBB	Baa	Adequate capacity to repay principal & interest. Slightly speculative.
BB	Ba	Speculative. Significant chance that issuer could miss interest payment.
B	Ba	Issuer has missed one or more interest or principal payments.
C	Caa	No interest is being paid on bond at this time.
D	D	Issuer is in default. Payment of interest or principal is in arrears.

In addition to the credit-worthiness ranking by the various services, bonds also fall into their own risk categories by broad type. There are essentially six types of bonds as they relate to risk.

1. Government. These securities all represent debts of the U.S. Government. Treasury securities are made up of treasury bills, which mature within a year; treasury notes, which mature between one and ten years; and treasury bonds, which mature from ten to thirty years. One of the advantages of treasury securities is that they are backed by the full faith and credit of the U.S. Government and the interest that they pay is tax-free on the state level. Government agency bonds are bonds sold by individual government agencies such as Fannie Mae. Technically, these are not backed by the full faith and credit of the United States but only the particular agency offering them. However, because it is highly unlikely the government would ever let one of its agencies default, these bonds are considered very secure. Investing in agency bonds allows you to get a little more return with little additional risk. The risk/reward difference is normally considered a good trade-off in this case.

2. **Municipals.** Municipal bonds pay interest that is tax-free on the federal level and tax-free to the residents of the state to which the bond is issued. This double tax savings makes them extremely attractive to investors in higher tax brackets. However, investors considering municipals should always do an analysis of their current tax bracket and the net return they would make investing in taxable bonds. If the return after taxes is higher, then there is no reason to invest in municipals unless you felt they were safer.

3. **Corporate bonds.** Corporate bonds are issued by individual corporations all around the world. These issues obviously vary in risk based on the stability of the companies offering the corporate bonds. The higher the stability, the lower the return offered. High return, low-rated bonds are referred to as junk bonds.

4. **Mortgages.** Mortgages on homes and even commercial properties are now packaged by banks and other primary lenders and sold off in large blocks to bond mutual funds. The more secure bonds have repayments of principal guaranteed on those bonds by a government agency such as the Government National Mortgage Association (GNMA), more commonly known as Ginnie Mae. If they are backed by the agency, then in fact they are backed by the U.S. Government. Consequently, the yield on such bonds will be lower than corporates but higher than a U.S. treasury bond.

5. **Convertibles.** Convertibles are a mix between bonds and stock. You own a debt instrument that pays you a stated interest, but you are allowed to convert that instrument to common stock if you desire to do so and under certain prescribed conditions. The advantage of a convertible is that they offer you a good return plus a potential upside should the value of the common stock increase. The disadvantage of a convertible is that they are more volatile than a straight bond.

6. **International bonds.** International bonds are made up of either corporate securities in other countries, or government securities of other countries. In addition to the normal risk associated with bond funds in the United States, the international bond funds are also subject to the additional risk of currency fluctuations. U.S. investors are sometimes misled by higher interest rate quotes without the understanding that converting the return back to U.S. dollars could reduce the overall yield.

PICKING THE SPECIFIC BOND FUND

After all is said and done, your two primary considerations for bond investing are risk and yield. Unless you are very conservative and investing in short-term bond funds, it is more likely that you will use bonds as either temporary holding investments that offer a higher yield than money markets or for specific purposes, such as to take advantage of falling interest or to buy tax-free income through municipals.

If you are buying municipal bonds in order to generate tax-free income, make sure you know your marginal tax bracket (see "What Is Your Tax Bracket," in Chapter 2) and continuously check the difference between taxable yields and tax-free yield on equivalent risk securities.

If you are investing in bonds to take advantage of falling interest rates, make sure you explore zero-coupon bonds. Investing in zero-coupon bonds as an "interest rate play" is an aggressive move because it can offer great returns in a short time—if you are right. For more information on zero-coupon bond funds, contact Benham Funds at 1-800-331-8331. This mutual fund family has the largest selection of zero-coupon treasury funds with good (low) expense ratios.

LET'S REMEMBER THIS:

► All bond funds are not the same.

► Bonds can have more risk than stocks.

► Bonds can be used to balance an overall investment portfolio.

▼

STRATEGIES TO REDUCE YOUR RISK

WHAT WE ARE GOING TO TALK ABOUT IN THIS CHAPTER:

- ► Risk Can be Reduced by Knowledge and Understanding
- ► The Lifestyle Phase of an Investor Helps Determine the Risk
- ► How to Periodically Adjust Your Risk

As I have implied throughout this book, in investing there is always a balance between acceptable risk and the return you will receive on your capital. While the amount of risk that is acceptable will vary tremendously between investors, it is important for you to learn ways that you can reduce risk and utilize those strategies when it least affects your return.

THE BETA FACTOR

One method of determining the risk of mutual funds is to compare their price volatility. If a fund is moving up or down compared to the rest of the market, that deviation is referred to as its volatility. Typically, a fund's price volatility is measured by comparing its own increase or decrease to a broader market, such as Standard & Poor's 500 or the New York Stock Exchange Common Stock Index. The broader the index, the more it represents the market as a whole.

For example, assume your fund has gained 18% this year while the New York Stock Exchange Common Stock Index gained 10%. Divide 10 into 18 and you get 1.8. This number, known as the Beta, represents the volatility factor for the individual fund compared to the market as a whole. The higher the Beta factor of the fund, the more aggressive it is compared to the overall market. By understanding Betas, you can quickly compare mutual funds to determine their aggressiveness and thus their comparative risk to other funds.

Using Beta factors, you can develop an investment strategy based around your risk tolerance. For example, you could invest in aggressive growth funds during rising markets and avoid them during falling markets. As a general rule, you would not want to stay in an aggressive growth fund during a down market. The reason is because many funds are using leverage and option techniques that would intensify a negative reaction in a down market. You want to get out of the aggressive funds when the market drops and either move into your temporary shelter, the money market fund, or a less aggressive fund. The use of Beta's would guide you to a lesser aggressive fund. The following table shows some well-known funds and their market Betas:

Table 8-1   Funds and Their Betas
(As measured against the S & P 500 Index)

Name	Beta
Fidelity Magellan	1.11
Fidelity Equity Income II	.84
Invesco Industrial Income	.74
Founder Special	1.31
Janus Worldwide	.89
Yachman	.92

Dollars & Sense: Use Betas to help determine a fund's volatility and potential risk.

ASSET ALLOCATION

Asset allocation is another way to reduce risk. The popular theory promotes dividing (allocating) your investments (assets) into several investment baskets, each with a different objective. This theory is normally promoted in conjunction with financial planning and changing your asset allocation model as your life cycle changes.

For example, in your early investment years (age 25 to 35), your are considered to be in your "wealth building" phase and should generally be more aggressive, placing 80% of your portfolio in stocks and 20% in bonds. In your later years (age 56+), you are generally in your "wealth preservation" stage and the reverse would be true: 20% in stocks and 80% in bonds. Somewhere between the two extremes of your life (age 36 to 55) you are in the "wealth enhancing" phase and you would actually balance at 50% bonds and 50% stocks (see Table 8-2). Interestingly, this 50/50% number is the one suggested by the late great investor Benjamin Graham in his classic stock investment book, *The Intelligent Investor,* as being the best long-term allocation of a person's investment portfolio.

Table 8-2   Asset Allocation

Three Phases of Wealth		
AGE	*PHASE*	*ASSET ALLOCATION*
25-35	Wealth Builder	80% stocks 20% bonds
36-55	Wealth Enhancement	50% stocks 50% bonds
56 plus	Wealth Preservation	20% stocks 80% bonds

There is certainly nothing wrong with Mr. Graham's theory. In fact, diversification—which is the more common term for asset allocation—is the guiding principle of mutual funds. On the other hand, I would be remiss if I didn't point out that there is a problem with too much diversification that people fail to consider. If, by diversifying, you throw out the potential for high returns and the low returns, then you are left with an average return and I don't like settling for average. However, if you feel most comfortable with this idea, then use asset allocation and also buy index funds. (See Chapter 9 for more information.) Your investment will be the epitome of "average."

And if that meets your investment return objectives, then that's precisely what you should do. On the other hand, if you can't get where you need to be financially on average returns, then you have a problem. This recognition of the investment law brings us back to our opening discussion. There is always a risk/reward ratio to investing. The more you attempt to protect your loss, the more upside potential you must surrender.

Another way to use asset allocation is to invest in mutual funds that automatically do that for you. These funds are called balanced funds. Unfortunately, not all balanced funds allocate assets the same and you must make sure that the one you select uses the techniques you agree with.

Just as you, as a single investor, can design an asset allocation model using different strategies, so can the fund. For example, the equity-oriented balanced fund will typically maintain from 55% to 65% of its portfolio in equities with the balance in investment grade bonds. A small portion of funds would be maintained in money markets. On the other hand, the income-oriented balance fund would normally maintain the opposite percentages of equity and bonds this time by placing the higher percentage in bonds. In this case, the stocks would also be selected based more on dividend yield. Frequently, utility stocks will be a large portion of the equity portfolios.

The third type of balanced fund is the asset allocation fund. In this fund, the manager takes a more active role in adjusting the portfolio mix according to the percentages he feels is justified by the current market. Obviously, this freedom to adjust the portfolio changes the risk rate as well as potential for gains. You are now relying more on the expertise of the manager reading and interpreting the economic conditions and less on the prudence of the balancing strategy itself.

If you don't use a balanced fund to do your asset allocation for you, don't forget to balance your assets every few years. The reason for this is that assuming you are doing well, one part of your portfolio will increase faster than the other. In order to maintain your planned allocation mix, you will need to sell off a portion of this portfolio and reposition the asset in the other part. If you don't do this, you defeat the whole purpose of asset allocation in the first place.

Dollars & Sense: Rebalance your investment portfolio every year or two to make sure you are still maintaining the investment allocation percentage you wanted to accomplish when you set up the plan.

I believe the traditional model of asset allocation is weighed too heavily toward bonds and that it has not yet been recalculated for the much greater lifespan that people have today. Active, knowledgeable investors in equity funds should be able to exceed bond fund performance at a greater ratio than a normal risk/reward standard. Consequently, I think you should increase your percentage of equity funds into later periods of your life. Additionally, I think some of the older views on asset allocation were unable to take into account the availability of different types of funds we have today. For example, any investor using asset allocation theories to reduce risk would likely include a blend of international funds to offset total exposure to U.S. markets. Equity holdings would also likely include some mix of index funds to provide future diversification. Figures 8-1A and 8-1B show a comparison between traditional asset allocation and modern asset allocation. Also, see Chapter 18, "Strategies For the Times of Your Life," for more examples.

DOLLAR-COST AVERAGING

Many of the best financial minds have concluded that because the stock market is in a constant state of fluctuation, it is very difficult for the average investor to "time" the market. These people promote the buy and hold approach. Additionally, they feel it is

Figure 8-1A Traditional Asset Allocation Model

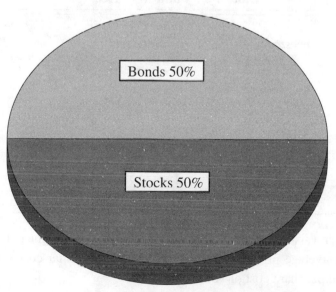

Figure 8-1B Modern Asset Allocation Model

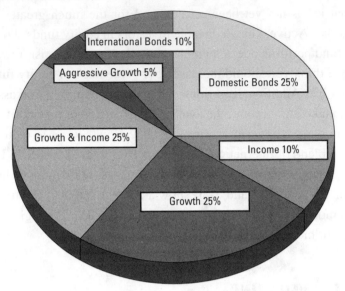

much better to make regular investment contributions in all types of markets as opposed to lump-sum contributions because the strategy will eventually save you money because some of your purchases will be at lower prices. This investment strategy is called dollar-cost averaging. The following table illustrates the way dollar-cost averaging (over a six-month period) is used to lower your investment cost.

		Table 8-3 **Fund X's Price**	
Month	*$ Invested*	*Value Per Share Net Asset*	*No. of Shares Purchased*
January	$100	$5	20.00
February	$100	$6	16.66
March	$100	$4	25.00
April	$100	$2	50.00
May	$100	$4	25.00
June	$100	$5	25.00
TOTAL	$600	$3.71 Avg. Price	161.66

Note that over a six-month period for a total of $600, you bought 161.66 shares of Fund X for an average price of $3.71. In this example, dollar-cost averaging has brought the true per share cost of your fund down.

The problem with pure dollar-cost averaging is that it promotes buying even during long market declines. If you do, you'll be buying even during periods where there are strong trends indicating lower prices ahead. I'm sure the stock brokers like that idea, but it doesn't make any sense at that point. Some readers will scoff at being able to spot a trend in prices that would indicate you're in a down market. To you, I would ask that you wait until the end of this book. By then, you too will be able to spot a trend.

For the record, I absolutely believe in systematic investing. Over time, systematic investing affords you the opportunity to add money and continuously compound your earnings. On the other hand, doing it blindly without regard to the current market or the economy at the time is to invest with blinders, throwing caution to the wind. Learn about the market trends and make them your friend, then use automatic investment plans during good markets and take a break during dry spells. For those of you who decide to use "dollar-cost averaging," consider using it with more aggressive funds than you might normally buy. The dollar-cost averaging will help reduce your overall risk and the fact that you now use a more aggressive fund could help increase your yield.

Money Talks: Dollar-cost averaging promotes continuous investing in the same stock at all price levels. Systematic investing promotes continuous investing, but uses different securities based on current market trends.

Automatic Investment Plans

Many funds now offer automatic investment plans so that you can take advantage of dollar-cost averaging or simply forced savings. Some funds can draft regular amounts out of your home bank and some even offer payroll deduction programs. I encourage everyone to take advantage of an automatic investment program during strong markets because it gives you the discipline that you might otherwise lack to invest regularly.

If it appears my encouragement for automatic investing conflicts with my position on dollar-cost averaging, it doesn't. Automatic investing should direct all your money into your fund's money market account. From the money market account you will decide when and where the money is invested in your other accounts in the fund family. Until you decide, the money will be sitting in a safe, if not perhaps lower-yielding money market, but you will have systematically continued your investment program.

Constant Dollar Plan

Like the other strategies we discuss to reduce risk, the constant dollar plan serves a purpose. In this case, the plan helps you determine whether now is the time to take profits or invest more. The plan concept is simple. Take a certain fixed dollar amount ($10,000, for example) that you want invested in a certain type of fund (aggressive) and maintain the balance. If the value is above $10,000 after the end of the first year, then you take the profits and put them in a money market fund. If the value is below $10,000 at the end of the year, then you take the money out of your money market fund and bring your aggressive portfolio back to $10,000.

For example, Table 8-4 shows how the constant dollar plan works. We have selected SteinRoe Capital Opportunities, an aggressive fund, and invested $10,000 on January 1, 1985, and $5,000 in a money market. Using the constant dollar plan you would have earned an annualized 8.23%. You have reduced your risk of investing directly into the aggressive fund and substantially increased your return over money market rates. On the other hand, had you invested in the aggressive fund for the entire period, your return would have been 14.67% annualized. Consequently, you gave up a higher return for a lower risk.

Table 8-4   Constant Dollar Plan

FUND: SteinRoe Capital Opportunities (SRFCX)				
Year	% Gain for year	Year End Money Fund Value	$ Amt +/- Money Mkt.	Year End Mkt. Balance[1]
			$10,000	$5,000
1986	16.77%	$11,677	$1,677	$6,877
1987	9.38%	$10,938	$938	$7,890
1988	-3.87%	$9,613	($387)	$7,543
1989	36.83%	$13,683	$3,683	$11,213
1990	-29.10%	$7,090	($2,910)	$8,450
1991	62.80%	$16,280	$6,280	$14,619

Year	% Gain for year	Year End Money Fund Value	$ Amt +/- Money Mkt.	Year End Mkt. Balance[1]
1992	2.42%	$10,242	$242	$15,108
1993	27.51%	$12,751	$2,751	$17,878
1994	0.00%	$10,000	$0	$18,593
1995	50.77%	$15,077	$5,077	$23,095
ANNUALIZED IRR = 8.23%				

[1] The year end money market balance equals the dollar amount added or deducted from the mutual fund performance plus an assumed 4% annualized gain.

LET'S REMEMBER THIS:

▶ Risk is a function of the product you buy, your individual goals, and your investment strategy. All of these variables can be adjusted to create an acceptable risk climate.

▶ A mutual funds risk can be determined by its historic volatility compared to the major indexes.

▶ Portfolios should be rebalanced at least annually to make sure the risk tolerance is still appropriate for your needs.

C H A P T E R 9

▼

HOW INDEX FUNDS CAN AVERAGE YOUR RISK

WHAT WE ARE GOING TO TALK ABOUT IN THIS CHAPTER:

▶ The Truth About the Buy and Hold Strategy

▶ How to Use Index Funds for Passive Investors

▶ How Broad Index Funds Can Diversify Your Investment

There are many people who believe that the best investment strategy is simply the "buy and hold approach." Pick the best stock or mutual fund based on a careful financial analysis and hold it for the long term. If you have read this book straight through, you will no doubt understand by now that I do not prefer this strategy. Anyone who holds a particular stock, mutual fund, or bond during all types of markets without regard to what is going on around them is simply not exercising prudent caution. This is not to say that jumping in and out of an investment is the right approach either. The true answer lies in an obvious blend of the two approaches. Select your investments wisely and hold until you have maximized your return compared to other present alternatives. Obviously, this is easier said than done and thus the reason they call it investing and not a guarantee.

Mutual funds offer an investment option that offers the long-term investor an opportunity to simplify the investment process. It isn't a panacea, but it is a viable opportunity for the more passive investor who has the mental ability to ride out bear markets or to spot them and make changes. That ability is an important qualifier for this strategy and is best used with longer holding periods. The type of fund I am discussing is an index fund.

Index funds have been around since Vanguard launched the first one in 1976 with only $11 million. Since then, their popularity has increased with the more recent longer-running bull markets. Now Vanguard's Index 500 Portfolio, which mirrors the Standard & Poor's 500 Index, has grown to $17.3 billion. To give you an idea of the number of index funds, I have provided a list in Table 9-1. Use this list also as a reference point to compare index funds and order prospectuses.

Table 9-1   Index Funds

American Gas Index Fund—Nat. Res.	800-343-3355
Benchmark Equity Index A—Equity	800-637-1380
Benchmark Small Company Index A—Equity	800-637-1380
Benchmark U.S. Treasury Index A—Bond	800-637-1380
Benham Global Natural Resources Index—Nat. Res.	800-331-8331
Biltmore Equity Index Fund—Equity	800-462-7538
BT Investment Institutional Equity 500 Index—Equity	800-949-9940
California Investment Trust S & P 500 Index—Equity	800-225-8778
California Investment Trust S & P Midcap—Equity	800-225-8778
Compass Capital Index Equity—Equity	800-451-8371
CoreFund Equity Index Fund—Equity	800-355-2693
Dreyfus Bond Market Index Fund Inv.—Bond	800-645-6561
Dreyfus Bond Market Index Fund R—Bond	800-645-6561
Dreyfus MidCap Index—Equity	800-645-6561
Dreyfus S & P 500 Index Fund—Equity	800-645-6561
Dreyfus Stock Index Fund—Equity	800-645-6561
Federated Index Max Cap (IS)—Equity	800-245-5051
Fidelity Inst. U.S. Bond Index—Bond	800-544-8888
Fidelity Inst. U.S. Equity Index—Equity	800-544-8888
Fidelity Market Index Fund—Equity	800-544-8888
First American Equity Index A—Equity	800-637-2548

First American Equity Index B—Equity	800-637-2548
First American Equity Index Inst.—Equity	800-637-2548
Galaxy Large Company Index—Equity	800-628-0414
Galaxy Small Company Index—Equity	800-628-0414
Galaxy U.S. Treasury Index—Bond	800-628-0414
Gateway Index Plus Fund—Equity	800-354-6339
Gateway Mid-Cap Index Fund—Equity	800-354-6339
Gateway Small-Cap Index Fund—Equity	800-354-6339
Harris Insight Index Fund—Equity	800-982-8782
Kent Index Equity—Equity	800-633-5368
Mainstay Equity Index Fund	800-522-4202
Mainstay Inst. EAFE Index—Equity	800-522-4202
Mainstay Institutional Index Bond—Bond	800-522-4202
Mainstay Institutional Index Equity—Equity	800-522-4202
Monitrend Summation Index Fund—Equity	800-251-1970
Munder Index 500—Equity	800-438-5789
Nations Equity Index Trust—Equity	800-321-7854
One Group Equity Index Inv.—Equity	800-338-4345
One Group International Equity Index—Foreign	800-338-4345
Portico Equity Index—Equity	800-228-1024
Prudential Inst. Stock Index—Equity	800-225-1852
Schwab International Index Fund—Foreign	800-526-8600
Schwab Small Cap Index Fund—Equity	800-526-8600
SEI Bond Index—Bond	800-342-5734
SEI S & P 500 Index—Equity	800-342-5734
Seven Seas S & P 500 Index—Equity	800-647-7327
Stagecoach Inst. Index Fund—Bond	800-222-8222
STI Classic International Equity Index—Foreign	800-428-6970
T. Rowe Price Equity Index Fund—Equity	800-638-5660
Vanguard Balanced Index Fund—Equity/Bond	800-662-7447
Vanguard Bond Index Intermediate-Term—Bond	800-662-7447
Vanguard Bond Index Long-Term—Bond	800-662-7447
Vanguard Bond Index Short-Term—Bond	800-662-7447
Vanguard Bond Index Total Bond Market—Bond	800-662-7447

continues

Table 9-1   Index Funds (continued)

Vanguard Index 500 Portfolio—Equity	800-662-7447
Vanguard Index Emerging Markets—Foreign	800-662-7447
Vanguard Index European Equity—Foreign	800-662-7447
Vanguard Index Extended Market—Equity	800-662-7447
Vanguard Index Growth—Equity	800-662-7447
Vanguard Index Small Cap Stock—Equity	800-662-7447
Vanguard Index Value—Equity	800-662-7447
Vanguard Institutional Index—Equity	800-662-7447
Victory Stock Index Fund—Equity	800-539-3863
Woodward Equity Index—Equity	800-688-3350

An index fund is a mutual fund that buys all of the stocks on a particular segment of the market. For example, one of the most common index funds is the Dow Jones Industrial Averages. This is an index based on 30 well-selected stocks that have historically been this country's gauge as to the direction of the stock market. An index mutual fund is made up of an equal investment in each of those thirty individual stocks creating a portfolio that mirrors the movement of the index. For example, if the Dow Jones Industrial Index goes up 20% a year and you have invested in the index mutual fund that follows the Dow Jones Industrial Average, your fund will correspondingly go up by 20%. Your personal return will be reduced by any fees paid in the mutual fund and taxes on capital gains. Naturally, the reverse is also equally true. Any decrease in the value of the index has a corresponding decrease in the value of that index mutual fund. The investment philosophy that follows this strategy is that if you believe the Dow Jones Industrial Average is going to go higher over a period of time, a good investment would be to invest in the Dow Jones Index instead of an individual stock or mutual fund that may perform better or worse than the overall index. This strategy centers on the theory that it is easier to predict the overall trend of the market than it is to pick an individual stock or mutual fund that will exceed or do better than the market.

The Dow Jones Index is certainly not the only index around. As index investing has become more well known and accepted, index mutual funds have been created on virtually every index available. There are indexes on value stocks, small capitalization stocks (Russell 2000 Index), mid-cap stocks, as well as the better known Standard & Poor's (S & P) 500, mentioned above, which is heavily weighed by stocks of companies with the largest market capitalization. These companies have traditionally represented over 60% of the total value of all U.S. common stock.

The broadest index is the Wilshire 5,000, which is composed of the stocks in the S & P 500 plus 4,500 other stocks. This index most closely represents the trend of the entire U.S. stock market and is thus a sounder standard of what is occurring to the market as a whole.

**Dollars &
Sense:** The broader the index, the more diverse your investment and the less it is subject to volatility.

For bond holders, there are mutual funds targeting the Lehman Bond Index, which is made up of virtually all investment grade bonds. The index has a portfolio duration of five years. Because there is a shorter term, the yield is lower, but it is more stable than a long-term bond fund. The Lehman Bond Index is characteristic of high-grade bonds and low expense.

International investors have their own alternatives for indices following the various markets. The two primary markets of Europe and the Pacific Basin have their own indices and one index follows the emerging market. By the time you read this book, there will likely be one index fund that ties all three areas of international investing together into an international super fund. Funds investing in an index will tend to have lower costs than funds investing in an individual country's stocks. Because international investing tends to have higher transactional costs than U.S. investing, the overseas mutual funds may be an important tool for the international investor.

**Dollars &
Sense:** Index funds allow passive investors to participate in the overall trend of the international market and reduce some risk of individual funds.

Index funds offer a big advantage to pension funds and other institutional investors who typically earn average returns because of their size. This is not because they don't know what they are doing with their money. Rather, it is because some have so much money they become over-diversified. Because of their size, they can't take advantage of niches in the market and the large account begins to gravitate towards the average return of the market. It is the equivalent of throwing out the highs and lows and only winding up with the mean. For these investors, the index funds offer a big savings through lower management costs. For example, Vanguard's S & P 500 has one of the lowest expense ratios of any index fund at .19%. On the other hand, in 1995, the average equity fund incurred expenses of 1.28%. With those expense ratios the average equity fund had to perform 1.09% better than the index fund just to stay even. For an individual investor that's not a lot of money, but for a pension fund it can add up to millions.

One advantage that both institutions and small investors will share by investing in index funds is the fact that there are few capital gain distributions. Because there is little trading in an index fund, all investors can save on annual taxes that are due from capital gain transactions normally incurred by a typical diversified equity fund. The result is that taxes are in large part totally deferred until you cash out. Additionally, because there is very little trading, there are very little expenses and transactional costs normally associated with mutual funds.

The major problem that I have with index funds is for the individual investor. Index funds fail to consider the psychology of the average investor, as well as the fact that bear markets exist. If you could be assured that the Dow Jones or the S&P 500 would continue to go up, then I would agree that investing in an index fund and leaving it would be a good strategy for people who did not want to spend the time or effort to research the best fund available. The use of the index fund would average out the risk in the stock market over a broad selection of stock. Unfortunately, the indices also participate in bear markets and go down in value. When the index you are following falls, so does the value of your investment. If you have invested in index funds because you are the kind of investor that does not want to spend time watching your investments, then you probably won't be watching it when the index begins to fall in value. If you aren't monitoring your investment, who's going to shift those dollars for you from the index fund to either a safe money market or a better performing fund? If no one is watching your investment, are you going to be comfortable if the index falls substantially in value? I don't think so, which is precisely why I raised the second problem of index investing. The profile of the individual investor, as opposed to institutional investor, who tends to choose an index fund because it will perhaps be more conservative in nature, is also the very individual who will get extremely nervous when the index drops in value. The result is an investor who jumps into and out of his index fund based on the ups and downs of the index. The investor is now attempting to utilize market timing, an entirely different market strategy requiring a different set of skills.

There is also another view of the fund expense issue as it relates to individual investors as opposed to institutional investors. While the statement is true that there are reduced fees, there is no more value in the argument of buying index funds to save fees than the one that suggests the "only" reason you should buy a no-load mutual fund is because you save on the commission charge in a loaded mutual fund. Saving money is important, but you shouldn't make your investment decisions simply on the fact that someone may or may not make a commission or on the fact that an index fund has a lower cost ratio than another fund. It seems like common sense to me that a fund producing a 15% average annual return with a cost ratio of 3%, yielding a total average annual return of 12%, is much better than an index fund, or any other fund, that is producing an average annual return of 10% but only has a cost of 1%. It seems clear to me that a 12% return beats a 9% return any day of the week, no matter what the investment. Consequently, while I think it is important to consider the expense of any fund, be it index, aggressive growth, or municipal bond, the reason for selecting it should not be based on the fact that the expense ratio is lower. The reason for selecting any investment should be based on overall return using a risk/reward comparison. If it doesn't meet that test, nothing else really matters.

The final reason suggested for investing in index funds is that it's fair to assume that over time indices will outperform half of the mutual funds and underperform half of the mutual funds, producing an average return for its investors. If you combine this return with lower transactional cost and low taxes (because of less trading), the result will be a higher net yield. To the passive investor, this argument may be acceptable. To the active investor, it only confirms his position. If you can't pick the better half of the mutual funds to invest in, you should be in another investment anyway.

In conclusion, let me say that index funds have a place for passive investors and large pension funds. On the other hand, if you are willing, able, and desirous of being an active investor, go for the premium that can be made from your efforts. Use the knowledge you are gaining in this book about the various mutual fund investing strategies to maximize your overall returns. A few extra percentage points each year over your investment life can make a dramatic difference in your retirement nest egg. Don't just take my word for it, look at Table 9-2 and see the difference just a few percentage points make over a period of years.

Table 9-2   Comparing Annual Compounded Returns

	$10,000 Investment		
Investment Time	*8% Return*	*10% Return*	*12% Return*
10 years	$22,196.40	$27,070.41	$33,003.87
20 years	$49,268.03	$73,280.74	$108,925.54
30 years	$109,357.30	$198,374.00	$359,496.41

Let's Remember This:

> ▶ Index funds are an excellent alternative for the passive investor.
>
> ▶ Index funds offer an excellent way to average your risk.
>
> ▶ Index funds offer full diversity to your portfolio.

▼

How the Economy & Interst Rates Effect Your Mutual Fund Return

What We Are Going to Talk About in This Chapter:

- ► How to Use Economics to Increase Your Returns
- ► How Interest Rate Cycles Determine the Best Investments
- ► How Inflation Hurts Your Investments

For years I have encouraged my clients and newsletter subscribers to keep one eye on the economy and one eye on their mutual funds. Specifically, I suggest that you chart the price movement of your mutual funds and make buy and sell decisions using moving averages viewed through the eyes of a fundamental economist. To a person who is a pure mutual fund technician and uses only charts to determine which funds are the best, this is hearsay. The reason is because I am suggesting you use economic data which is fundamental market analysis to help you interpret your technical charts, something the technical analyst thinks impossible. Nevertheless, the combined approach is particularly helpful to determine whether a change in a particular fund's price trend is likely to be a short-term or a long-term change. Matching new economic data to a fund's historic price chart gives the reader an added insight into what is to come, not just what has been. Fundamentalists criticize this analysis as being akin to reading tea leaves, but that is also unfair and biased.

In Bill Clinton's 1992 presidential campaign, one slogan was frequently used by his staff. "It's the economy, stupid." The slogan was used to remind everyone on the campaign staff that they needed to continuously repeat their economic message to an audience frightened of the current state of affairs. The slogan is also apropos to those of us who try to analyze what is happening in the stock market and in which direction it is likely to move. The reason for this is that the stock market is really made up of the corporations whose stock is sold on the exchanges. If the general economy that these corporations operate is either positive or negative, it will effect the profits of every corporation. Sooner or later that effect will be reflected in the price of a particular company's stock. When the economic changes will effect any particular corporation is the element that chartists attempt to decide by viewing their trend charts.

Economics 101

Mutual funds are made up of their underlying instruments such as stocks or bonds. If you are investing in an equity mutual fund, whatever forces effect the underlying value of the stocks in a portfolio will in turn effect the value of the mutual fund.

As a basic premise, it is both rational and reasonable to say that ultimately (not daily, weekly, or even monthly) the price of a stock will be directly related to the value of the company. Equally true, we can say that the value of a company at any time is affected one way or the other by external factors within the economy. That is why a very successful company's stock will fall when there is no justification for this based upon the company's income and expenses. Some external factor has affected the perception that the buying public has for the stock of that particular company.

While economic factors have a varying effect on individual companies, they will have a dramatic effect on the value of the market as a whole. Thus, while looking at the economy may help us understand a particular stock's potential course, it is most helpful in determining the overall direction of the market as a whole. If you have a good understanding of where the overall market is heading then you can determine whether your money should be in stock equities, bonds, or sitting safely on the sidelines in money markets. This theory is the essence of economic timing and should be understood by all investors. The major reason for its importance is the understanding that most of the money made in the market is made in periods of market spurts. If you are out of the market during these periods of time, and invested instead in money markets, you will lose a large portion of the potential profits that you can make in the stock market. In fact, this is the very reason fundamentalists say market timing is a poor theory.

Dollars & Sense: Use the direction of the economy to decide whether to be in stocks, bonds, or money markets.

INTEREST RATES AND THE MARKET

Most companies have debt. Successful companies use it for expansion and less successful ones use it to stay afloat. In either case, interest paid on that debt is generally a large percent of the company's overall expense. Because much of a company's debt is tied to variable interest rates, the interest rates on a company's loan rises with the adjustments by the Federal Reserve of short-term interest rates. A rise in short-term interest rates means higher payments for the company and that results in more expense for the company and less profits. If a company's profits fall because of the increase, the price of its stock ultimately decreases. The reverse of this is equally true. If interest rates fall, a company with debt has that portion of its expenses go down, profits go up and the price of the company's stock improves. These events aren't necessarily immediately reflected in the value of the stock, but ultimately it must be.

Dollars & Sense: When interest rates fall, the stock market rises. This is when investors should have their funds in equity stocks or bonds.

While there are certainly many variables that effect a given company's profit, the rule just expressed effects those companies with debt. And because that includes most of the companies that make up the stock market, rate changes effect the market as a whole. Thus, when short-term rates are falling, the overall market tends to do well because the company's that make up the market are experiencing higher profits. The bond market also does well during this period because the price of existing bonds increases in value as interest rates fall on new bonds being offered. The reason for this is because investors are willing to pay more for older bonds that have the higher yield.

How about long-term rates? Long-term rate changes are a better aid for us to judge the direction of the market. The main reason is because the direction of long-term rates is a key indicator of the direction of inflation. It isn't so much that the change in long-term rates is having an effect on the market as it is the understanding that falling long-term rates are occurring because the Federal Reserve believes that inflation is under control or falling. To keep the economy from falling into a recession, the Fed lowers interest rates and makes loans more readily available. This pumps new cash into the marketplace which results in more goods and services being purchased.

Falling rates will also cause the stock market to rise because the market will interpret the decrease in rates as a signal that the Fed feels inflation is under control. The one factor that the market reacts most positively to is a decrease in inflation. The reason is that if inflation is low, the value of your corporate earnings improves. If interest rates also fall, your corporate expense falls. Ultimately, these two factors will yield higher corporate profits and in turn higher stock prices.

Rising interest rates also effect the market, but the negative implications may not be long term and markets can perform well with rising rates. For example, because so many major institutional investors follow interest rates, a quick shift in direction will cause the stock market to react negatively. This reaction may be short-lived and will not establish a new market trend if increases in inflation don't occur as well. This occurs because a moderate increase in interest rates due to a moderate economic growth (growth without inflation) is actually good for the economy because the individual companies will prosper in other ways, such as increased sales. The company's bottom-line profits will be increased more than the interest rate increase has raised expenses. A company will be hurt only when the growth is accompanied by higher and higher cost of goods (inflation) which in turn reduces profit.

Dollars & Sense: Rising inflation and rising interest rates will foretell a bad stock market ahead.

WHICH RATES TO WATCH

Short-term rates are more erratic and it is very difficult to make decisions based on these movements. Long-term rates, such as the 30 year treasury securities or the 30 year AAA corporate bond index, are a good measure and the easiest to use for most investors. A quick glance at the chart below (Figure 10-1) will let you see the inverse relationship of these two indicators.

Figure 10-1   Interest Rate v. Dow Composite

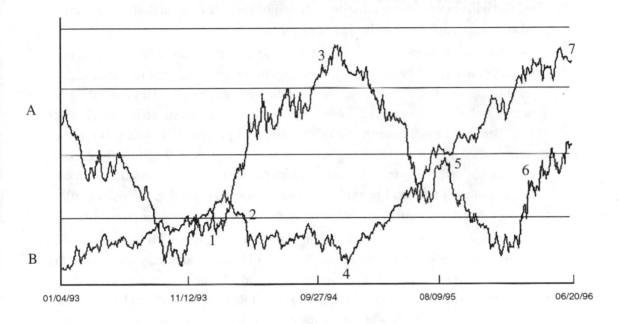

In our charts we use the market as measured by the Dow Jones Composite Index and the U.S. Treasury Bond 30 year Index to represent interest rates. The line labeled A is the long-term interest rate and the line labeled B is the Dow composite. Note first that as rates began to fall in 1993, the market improved. When rates reversed their course (point 1), the market very shortly did the same (point 2). At the height of interest rates (point 3), the market was at its lowest (point 4). Immediately as rates shifted down, the market moved up. A slight rise in rates at point 5 was too short to slow the market although there was a minor dip. At point 6, the rates are rising and you can see that the market is slowing at point 7. This is the point we are at as I write this chapter. The rise in rates has slowed, but the increase has also slowed the market. If rates fall, the market will continue up. If rates continue up, the market will fall back. My question to you as you read this book is, was I correct?

Real Interest Rates

For those of you who wish to be more precise in your research, the best indicator is the "real" rate of interest. The real rate of interest is determined by subtracting an inflation value from current long-term interest rates. The reason that this is a better comparison is because it takes into consideration the effects of inflation on money cost. You will remember that inflation is the major variable in the action of the overall market so it is helpful to use this factor in our calculation.

For calculation purposes, we will use the Produce Price Index (PPI) as our inflation number and the 30 year Treasury Securities Index for our interest rate number. To determine the "real" rate of interest, subtract the PPI rate from the Treasury rate. For example, if the Treasury rate is 7% and the PPI is 4%, then the real interest rate is 3%. If you then compare the movement of that rate along a time line, you will see the direction of "real" interest rates and consequently the expected direction of the market. If you have a situation where your real interest rate is negative, inflation is on the move and interest rates will be raised to counterbalance. Likewise, the rise in inflation and interest rates will cause the stock market to perform poorly in the future.

For those of you who may be wondering how to practically benefit from all of this, it's simple. It is easier to determine the direction of interest rates than it would be to judge the direction of the stock market if you didn't know to watch rates. This is because interest rates are controlled by the Federal Reserve and although they never tell you in advance exactly what they are going to do, they are always giving strong indications. Again, its no guarantee but when you have a fund that is performing well and you are reasonably comfortable that rates aren't rising, it's an excellent opportunity to let your profits run and even add more money. If you begin to see that interest rates are starting to rise, it will be a strong indication to start paying close attention to the market again.

Dollars & Sense: Use real interest rates as the best predictor of the future of the market.

The Inflation Factor

Earlier I said that inflation was the real Wall Street killer and that interest rates were just the symptom. Many people follow interest rates because they are widely published and easy to follow. If you would like to go to the heart of the matter you can look directly at the trend in commodity prices to determine the direction of inflation.

The most common measure of inflation is the Consumer Price Index (CPI). This compares the retail price paid by the consumer for a group of goods and services. It is widely reported in all national financial publications as well as CNBC.

Another gauge of inflation that may be more accurate for your purpose is the Produce Price Index (PPI). It is better because it shows the early stage of inflation. The PPI reflects the cost of the goods at the producer level as opposed to the consumer level. It is sort of an advanced warning of what the consumer is about to experience in the coming months. Interestingly, the difference between these two indices (price paid by producer and price paid by consumer) is the profit of American companies. Following the trends of these indicators will give you some very good information on the direction of inflation as well as the direction of corporate profits in America. As the profits of companies go up or down, so does the direction of their stock prices. Generally, there is only a few month's lag time between the two events.

Dollars & Sense: An increasing Produce Price Index (PPI) is bad for the stock market and a decreasing PPI predicts a good market ahead.

Unemployment Numbers

The third indicator that will help you determine the overall direction of the stock market is the unemployment number. This statistic is released on the second Friday of every month by the U.S. Labor Department and will be announced on the evening news.

The unemployment numbers tend to throw people off because the statistic sounds like a double negative. When unemployment is going down, most people view that as good news and that is certainly the way it is presented by the national newscaster. Unfortunately, full employment (low <u>un</u>employment) is actually bad for the stock market. The reason is because to have full employment the economy has to be raging at full capacity. That means wages are on the rise, prices are on the rise (inflation) and the stock market will be falling because the economy will have no place else to go but down.

On the other hand, when unemployment is rising the stock market will tend to do well because inflation will be forced down, interest rates will fall to help avoid a recession, and corporate profits rise as we have already discussed.

Naturally, there are extremes to all of these rules and that is what many people focus on. The continued extension of high unemployment is first recession and then depression. Neither of these factors would be good for the economy. Consequently, what we are looking for is a gentle balance, the proverbial "soft landing" that you hear the local nightly newscaster hoping for. While the market won't do well in that arena either, the next trend is up.

Dollars & Sense: Low unemployment (high employment) predicts an increase in inflation and lower stock prices ahead.

Summary

Economic indicators are no panacea for following the stock market. If they were precise, everyone would know exactly when to buy and sell. Instead, what these indicators are is another tool to help you determine the market's direction. Like anything, the more you use the tool the better you become at understanding how it can be used and its shortfalls. The better you become at using the tool, the more easily you are able to make adjustments in your investments based upon your experience.

Let's Remember This:

▶ When interest rates are falling the stock market generally rises.

▶ In a falling interest rate environment bonds increase in price.

▶ The Produce Price Index (PPI) is a forecaster for the future direction of stock prices.

▼

CHAPTER 11

THE PROFITLINE STRATEGY

WHAT WE ARE GOING TO TALK ABOUT IN THIS CHAPTER:

► There is No Perfect Long-term Investment

► How Moving Averages Can Help You Make Buy and Sell Decisions

► The Effect of Relative Strength as a Buy/Sell Indicator

As we approach the new century, our economy is once again changing. Corporate restructuring is causing new worker concerns about their economic future. Additionally, as the population ages more people are concerned about retirement and the obvious void they see between the money they will need and the money they are saving.

With this changing environment also comes changes in the stock market. Volatility has become more of a norm than an exception. Even the once stable bond markets now fluctuate with the frequency of equity markets. This new fluctuation adds concern to the traditional, more conservative bond buyer.

To the novice investor, turbulent times create uncertainty. Because the new investor is unsure of his action, he chooses not to invest in the stock market. Unfortunately, that means a loss of a potentially big opportunity. Although 1995 was expected to be a weak year for the stock market and equity funds, it proved just the opposite. Investors who stayed in the market attained terrific gains. The real losers were those who sought safety and stayed in money markets and CDs. This year only added to investors' confusion because the previous year, 1994, had flipped the other way. Just when everyone thought it safe to go back into the market, its performance lagged and created a great deal of investor frustration.

The question for all investors is, "How can I invest my money with reduced risk following a plan that eliminates the guesswork?"

While I do believe a client should maximize his or her monies by being invested in the market, I am not particularly impressed by traditional buy and hold strategies. Through years of personal research and investments, I have concluded that risk-averse investment growth requires some method of "timing" the mutual fund, stock, and bond markets in order to maximize return with reduced risk. Timing the market means following a plan to be invested in the market during uptrends, and out of the market and into money markets during declines.

The investment strategy that has resulted from this philosophy is known as "market timing." This strategy searches for long-term trends in the market's constant fluctuations. During perceived uptrends in the market, investments are positioned in securities to achieve the greatest return. When the market appears to have reached a significant peak, investments are moved into money markets until the next uptrend occurs.

Money Talks: Market timing is a strategy of always trying to be invested "in" the market during uptrends and "out" of the market during downtrends.

With the development of today's computer technology and the accessibility of a plethora of market and economic data, timing has become easier for the individual investor to perform as well as for the professional.

"The Buy and Hold Theory"

Since the formation of stock markets, investors have continuously sought ways to avoid down markets, while benefiting from market gains. The traditional theory of investing says that you buy a top-performing security based on historical performance and hold onto it. Over the years, as the theory goes, your investment should balance out the highs and lows, leaving you with a reasonable gain. Using this theory, the average stock mutual fund has yielded around 12%, and the average bond fund between 7.55% and 8.45%. At first glance, this appears to be an acceptable approach to many people because they would be happy with that type of return. The problem is that even if that were an acceptable return, the numbers you are looking at are "the average." You can make most investment theories look good if you use the average because you have guaranteed within your premise that the investor didn't make a mistake and pick any one of the lower half of the mutual funds that did below average. That's quite an assumption. Additionally, if you take this theory to its logical conclusion, you would only buy index funds because they are the true average of the market and you would hold them forever. While I'm sure there are some who would now be saying "That's exactly right," it's not and I'll explain why. Because there are now virtually thousands of mutual funds, the buy and hold theory tells you that half of those are going to do worse than the average.

Even if we assume that you had picked a fund that has historically been a winner, there are numerous factors that could change its performance, such as:

1. Fund managers can retire or switch to new fund families.

2. Fund managers make mistakes.

3. Fund objectives can change or become outdated.

4. Bear markets bring almost all funds down.

5. The best performing funds become popular, thus larger and more difficult to manage and continue previous performances.

It is also important to note that the returns previously mentioned are for a certain time period. The problem with using arbitrary periods is that they don't take into account an individual and your personal circumstances which are always changing. If you change the time period because of your own facts and circumstances, you might find that unbeknownst to you, your purchase of a fund was at its historic high, from which it doesn't recover for years. Additionally, because our financial lives are such that we can't hold forever, you might have to sell at the bottom of a market. In either of these cases, your average as opposed to the market average could reflect a loss.

THE PROFITLINE STRATEGY

Let me ask you a question. What would happen if you were invested in the stock market primarily when prices were rising and were safely positioned in money market funds when the market experienced substantial declines? Ideally, you would experience superior returns of the stock market over other investments, have less fluctuation of your investments, know that you could liquidate your investments at any time and, most importantly, you would spend less time worrying about your financial assets and more time on the things you enjoy in life. By avoiding weak periods in the market and participating in the strong, you can experience superior returns over the traditional buy-and-hold strategy while also reducing risk by limiting your investment's downside.

There are numerous possible methods for determining when to buy and sell the markets. Most methods are devised by looking at data and charts of what has happened consistently in the past, and then waiting for that set of circumstances to repeat itself again in the future when you can take action on it. This is typical of market timing techniques. However, pitfalls for investors abound with most market timing methods because:

1. They take a lot of time to implement and monitor, and most people today don't have the required time.

2. As times change and markets become driven by different forces, some methods become outdated and no longer perform as well.

In an attempt to minimize your risk as well as maximize your returns, I have constructed a strategy that does not depend on political or economic events to make it work. It is simple and takes the emotion out of making an investment decision. Most importantly, it works. It is called the PROFITLINE STRATEGY and it is based on two historically sound concepts: (1) moving averages, and (2) relative strength momentum.

MOVING AVERAGES

As you know, an average is a simple mathematical calculation to find the mid-point of a group of numbers. A moving average, as it relates to the stock market, is an average based on the closing prices for a stock, bond, or mutual fund over a period of days or weeks.

The best way to follow the price of any mutual fund and its moving average is to use a fund price range chart. The price range chart displays the range (high to low) that the price of a mutual fund traded in during a particular week. It also shows the final (closing) price for that week.

When weeks of data are displayed on a price range chart, the chartist may visually detect patterns or trends that have taken, or are still taking, place. The chart below for *Fidelity Equity Income II* for May 1993 through May 1996 will aid us in my discussion of the Profitline Strategy. (See Figure 11-1.)

Money Talks: A price range chart is a graph that shows a line made by connecting daily points that represent the price of a security. When the dots are connected the line that is produced is called the price line.

The irregular line (labeled 1) in the graph is the actual net asset value (NAV) of the *Fidelity Equity Income II* fund. Please note the second line (labeled 2), in general, follows the actual price line. This second line is the graph of the 15-week moving average for the *Fidelity Equity Income II*. The third line (labeled 3) is the 39-week moving average for the fund. It is the relationship of these lines and their importance to your investment return that helped us coin the name *"Profitline."*

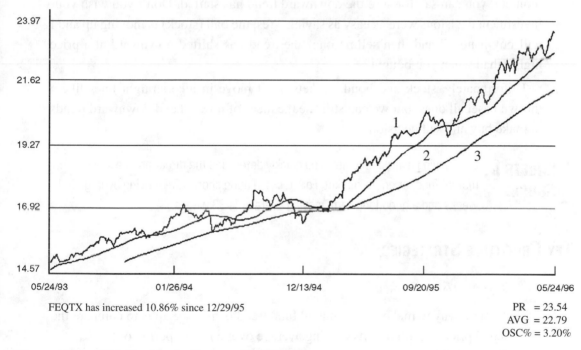

FEQTX has increased 10.86% since 12/29/95

PR = 23.54
AVG = 22.79
OSC% = 3.20%

Figure 11-1 Fidelity Equity Income II (FEQTX)

The reason the Profitline Strategy has worked is because it does not depend on a particular economic event, or any market rumors. Buy and sell decisions within the Profitline Strategy are based solely on the price movement of the market, the price movement of a particular mutual fund, and the fund's relative strength momentum (RSM) compared to other funds.

The best way to simplify why this strategy works is to remind ourselves of some basic laws of physics. (I promise this will be easy!) "An object in motion (in a certain direction tends to) stay in motion (in that direction)." Now, the financial markets are hardly as simple as tossing a baseball up in the air, but the principle is easy to see by visualizing a ball thrown into the air.

When you see a ball being thrown upward, you naturally assume that a moment later the ball will be higher than it was the moment before. In fact, you continue to assume the ball will move higher in altitude until when? When the force of gravity acts on the ball to push it in a downward direction, right?

But think about it. You can't see the gravity, so how do you know for sure that the ball has stopped in its upward track and is now headed down? Easy question, isn't it? When you see the ball physically lower in one moment as compared to the previous moment, you can say for sure the downward trend has started. Don't you wish your investment decisions were as easy as saying "Yes, the ball (stock) is moving up and I will buy it now," and then selling once the trend has shifted downward at a price higher than when you bought?

Unfortunately, stock and bond markets don't move in nice straight lines like a thrown baseball does, but we can still use the ideas of upward and downward trends to make buy and sell decisions.

> **Dollars & Sense:** Use moving averages to help you quickly determine the direction of a stock, bond, mutual fund, or entire market. For stocks, a good short-term moving average is 15 weeks and a good long-term moving average is 39 weeks.

KEY PROFITLINE STRATEGIES

1. *Buy into rising markets.*

   A sound way to make sure a mutual fund trend is moving up is to compare the actual price of a fund to its moving average over a recent period of time. (Based on historical performance, we have selected a 39-week moving average as our main reference point.) The moving average serves as your "last moments" reference and the actual price is your current moment.

   If the actual price is above the moving average line, the trend is still considered to be "up" and the security is rated a "buy" (although profits can be maximized by purchasing at just the right time, as we'll discuss later).

2. *Sell when trend has shifted down.*

If and when the actual price of a stock or bond drops below the moving average, the trend should be considered "down." If this particular security is owned, it should be sold as quickly as possible.

The optimum time to make these buy and sell decisions is as soon as the uptrend or downtrend has been established. Remember that the trend is consid ered established at the point in time when the actual price line crosses the moving average in either the up (buy) or down (sell) direction.

As an investor, you must watch for these points to occur, and then take action by buying or selling as indicated by the Profitline Strategy.

Let's look again at the *Fidelity Equity Income II* fund graph for May 1993 to May 1996 (see Figure 11-2). Note the arrows which have been labeled "B" for buy and "S" for sell, and how they indicate the points where the actual price line crosses the moving average line. The buy signal in this case is actually at a higher price than when the fund was previously sold at the point labeled "S." While some investors might be confused as to why you would buy a fund at a higher price than you previously sold it, the reason is the trend. You sold it when the trend was going down and you bought it back when the trend was reversed and moving up.

While this chart created an inconvenient trade, it more importantly protected your downside risk yet immediately got you back into the market to profit from the long rise. This chart has been purposely used because it illustrates the main criticism of moving averages (that you will sometimes be taken out of the market when you could have remained) but it also shows that the minor inconvenience has a big tradeoff—downside protection.

When a sale is made of a fund you are holding, the proceeds from that sale should have one of two dispositions:

1. Transfer directly to a money market mutual fund to earn interest while those funds are "out" of the market.

2. Transfer to another mutual fund if one of the funds you are monitoring is currently at a position that the Profitline Strategy rates as a "buy." One note of

Figure 11-2 Fidelity Equity Income II (FEQTX)

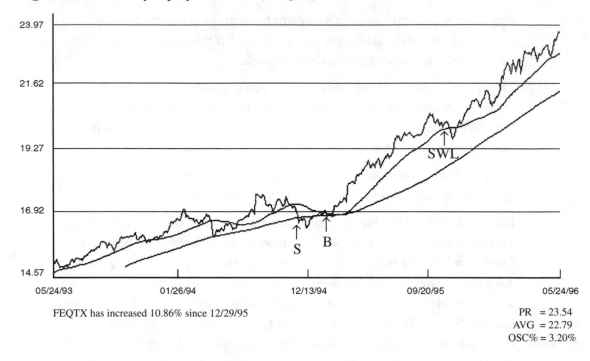

FEQTX has increased 10.86% since 12/29/95

PR = 23.54
AVG = 22.79
OSC% = 3.20%

caution: It will be tempting to switch from fund to fund to always be in the market. We recommend patience as an investor. Don't be afraid to sit in a money market fund for awhile if nothing else looks good. Don't be greedy because you might fall into a trap that is summed up with this old Wall Street adage:

Bulls make money, bears make money, pigs get slaughtered!

The Profitline Strategy will allow you to buy stocks, bonds, or mutual funds after an uptrend has been confirmed (by the actual price moving above that of the moving average) and sell those same investments if and when the uptrend stops and a downtrend begins (as signaled by the actual price dropping below the moving average price).

Sounds easy right? Well, it definitely isn't hard, but there are more details to discuss and learn in order to maximize your results using the Profitline Strategy.

Most important in the Profitline Strategy is the selection of the length of the term of the moving average that you select to use as your reference. Always remember that a short-term moving average, meaning one with less data included in the calculation, will be more aggressive and result in more trades occurring as the market cycles up and down in its normal daily and weekly pattern.

Dollars & Sense: The Profitline Strategy uses a long-term, 39-week moving average to provide stability and safety. In addition, we use a more aggressive, 15-week moving average to provide an early warning system.

The reason that short-term moving averages are more aggressive is that each individual data point makes up a large percentage of the total input to the moving average. Thus, a short-term moving average will move more for a given change in the actual price of a security as compared to a long-term average.

For example, a 10-week moving average contains 10 data points in the calculation. Each data point represents 10% of the total. This is a significant portion of the total when compared to a commonly used long-term average like the 39-week moving average where each data point represents about 2.6% (1/10 = 10%, 1/39 = 2.6%).

To you, the chartist and investor, the importance of this latest lesson is to realize that short-term moving averages (when plotted on a chart) will very closely follow the actual price line. The consequence of this effect is something called "whipsaw."

Whipsaw occurs when the actual price line is close to the moving average line and crosses it temporarily without a change in the direction of the trend. Figure 11-3 shows a whipsaw in action. Let me explain how it occurs.

Previously, you purchased shares of the XYZ fund because the actual price moved above the 10-week moving average, signaling an uptrend. Two weeks later, rumors of the President being seriously ill cause the market to drop 3% and the XYZ fund drops below the 10-week moving average line which was trailing closely due to its short term. You sell your shares of the XYZ fund because you believe a downtrend has started. Due to the short time you were in the market, you could possibly lose a small amount on your investment, or maybe be lucky enough to make a small amount. The next day, the rumors prove to be false, the market rises 2% and the XYZ fund goes back up above its moving average, forcing you to purchase it again at a higher price than you just sold at the previous day. You have been whipsawed!

The best method to minimize whipsaw is to use long-term moving averages. With the larger base of data found in the longer term average, the average moves a little slower and, in general, won't put you into the market unless a stronger uptrend is in place. You won't be able to eliminate whipsaw as our example of *Fidelity Equity Income II* shows, but you can minimize it.

Figure 11-3 Fidelity Equity Income II (FEQTX)

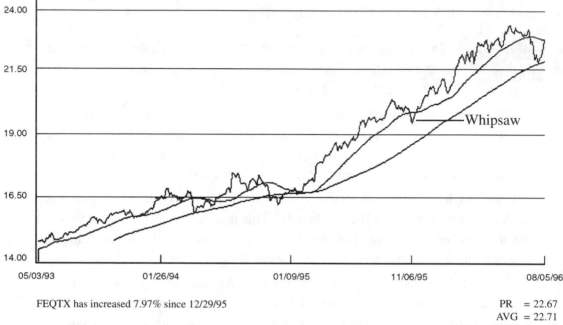

FEQTX has increased 7.97% since 12/29/95

PR = 22.67
AVG = 22.71
OSC% = -0.17%

Another consideration against using short-term averages for your major decision line is the increased number of trades that will occur. Many mutual fund families restrict the number of switches that you can make in a given time period and frequent trading may cause the fund to cancel your privilege. In addition, if you were using the Profitline Strategy to trade individual stocks and bonds, you might be paying commissions each time you buy and sell. These fees can equal or exceed your profits when short-term trading. This is another one of the main reasons I recommend you use "no-load" mutual funds.

The 39-week moving average has proven to be an excellent length of term for the intermediate- to long-term investor. Use of the 39-week moving average allows trends to establish prior to your making a buy or sell decision and, for most funds or securities, results in a maximum of one or two trades per year.

What would have happened during the crash of 1987 using the Profitline Strategy? If you were using the 39-week moving average of that particular index to make your overall market decision, it would have sold you out of the market at a level of 2,350 in the long decline from 2,722 which finally ended at the 1,730 level. This is the safety feature the Profitline Strategy gives you.

The Profitline Strategy goes one step further in identifying buy and sell points. A watch-list should be maintained containing those mutual funds that have crossed their 15-week moving average. The 15-week moving average will usually be crossed prior to the decision-making 39-week moving average because it will follow the actual price line more closely due to its short-term nature. Once the fund's price crosses its short-term moving averages by moving down in trend, it is subject to potential sale. Conservative investors could initiate a sale if general market conditions were also deteriorating. This could be confirmed by using the 39-week moving average of the market as illustrated by the Dow Jones, Composite Index, or S & P 500 index.

Two watch-lists are maintained, a buy watch-list (BWL) for funds that are moving upward toward their 39-week moving average, and a sell watch list (SWL) for those funds dropping toward their 39-week moving average. If and when the funds on the "buy" or "sell" watch-list continue their trend and cross their 39-week moving average, the fund is moved to the buy action list (BAL) or sell action list (SAL).

The action list is the list you have in your hand when you call your mutual fund company to give them instructions to buy or sell your positions. For an example of how this works in practice, refer to Figure 11-4. Notice at the point marked SWL the price line crosses down and through the short-term moving average line. This created

Figure 11-4 Fidelity Equity Income II (FEQTX)

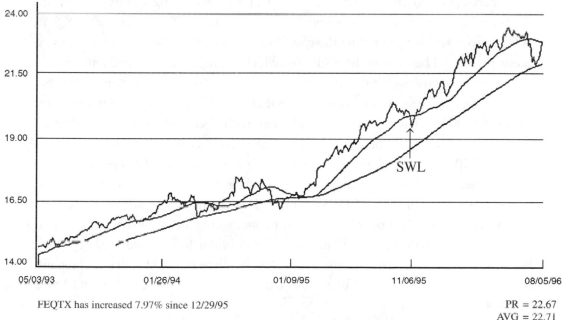

FEQTX has increased 7.97% since 12/29/95

PR = 22.67
AVG = 22.71
OSC% = -0.17%

a sell warning. Had the price line continued down through the long-term moving average, we would have sold. Fortunately, however, the fund improved and moved back above its short-term moving average and we remained fully invested.

RELATIVE STRENGTH MOMENTUM

The second part of the Profitline Strategy involves the use of a fund's relative strength momentum (RSM). RSM is the comparisons of the performance of a particular fund and others within its peer group to a market index. For example, if *Fidelity Equity Income II* is performing at an average return of 12% and the general market, as exemplified by the S & P 500, is producing a 9% annual return, the RSM of *Fidelity Equity Income II* would be better than the market and therefore a candidate for purchase.

Dollars & Sense: Use Relative Strength Momentum (RSM) to quickly compare funds to see which ones are doing better than the overall market.

In order to see RSM put into practice, let's walk through an example. Suppose that in May of 1996 you decide to invest in an aggressive growth mutual fund. You have opened a trading account with Charles Schwab and you are going to use their mutual fund marketplace to select your funds. Table 11-1 shows the 62 aggressive growth funds available, their returns for 1 year, 90 days and 30 days. The return for the S & P 500 is also listed. By comparing the chart, we see that 36 of the aggressive growth funds performed better than the S&P 500, which is ranged at number 37 in performance over the past twelve months. Out of those funds, the top three funds over the last 90 days are Perkins Opportunity (POFDX), SteinRoe Capital Opportunity (SRFCX), and Heartland Small-Cap Contrarian (HRSMX). From an RSM standpoint, any of these three would be good purchase candidates because their current performance is still strong. The final aid for our selection is the past 30 day's performance. In this case, they all have given back some of their gains. However, of the three, I would select SteinRoe Capital Opportunities. This is a judgment call but its performance was the very best over the one year period, second in the 90-day period, and second of our final three in the 30-day period. Any of the three would be acceptable, but strictly on this one criteria I would pick the SteinRoe Fund. In actuality, I would put all three through the rest of our testing, but the SteinRoe Fund would have the lead.

Table 11-1   VersaRank(tm) of Ntf-aggr list

	Ranking by column 1 for date 06/21/96		
	Since 06/21/95	Since 03/21/96	Since 05/21/96
1 SRFCX	+62.35%	+13.85%	-4.96%
2 IAEGX	+51.36%	+7.67%	-8.77%
3 PBEGX	+46.99%	+9.21%	-9.95%
4 BESCX	+45.98%	+12.94%	-6.39%
5 VSEAX	+45.61%	+11.52%	-3.36%
6 PBHGX	+44.58%	+5.84%	-7.26%
7 BTSCX	+42.01%	+5.97%	-13.18%
8 ACAPX	+41.75%	+5.75%	-7.30%
9 WAEGX	+41.10%	+11.13%	-2.70%
10 POFDX	+40.41%	+14.04%	-6.68%
11 BARAX	+40.21%	+7.91%	-2.09%
12 KAUFX	+37.52%	+8.84%	-4.98%
13 SRSVX	+34.83%	+9.13%	-2.33%
14 GSCQX	+34.43%	+9.08%	-10.63%
15 SKSEX	+32.48%	+12.00%	-0.82%
16 FDISX	+32.33%	+9.03%	-10.28%
17 EAGAX	+31.33%	+6.61%	-4.65%
18 CUEGX	+31.23%	+4.74%	-6.89%
19 MNMCX	+30.97%	+9.75%	-6.11%
20 FIEGX	+30.71%	+3.14%	-12.29%
21 NBGNX	+29.36%	+7.04%	-1.46%
22 DGAGX	+29.05%	+4.72%	+0.70%
23 ARTSX	+28.82%	+3.95%	-5.55%
24 HRSMX	+28.79%	+13.36%	-1.34%
25 FIDYX	+28.54%	+2.87%	-3.75%
26 FOUNX	+27.75%	+6.29%	-3.52%
27 SPEQX	+27.10%	+7.00%	-3.72%
28 HRTVX	+26.39%	+7.19%	-1.22%

continues

Table 11-1   VersaRank(tm) of Ntf-aggr list (continued)

	Ranking by column 1 for date 06/21/96		
	Since 06/21/95	*Since 03/21/96*	*Since 05/21/96*
29 DNLDX	+26.20%	+6.33%	-3.70%
30 ACRNX	+24.86%	+7.09%	-2.51%
31 RSEGX	+24.61%	+11.83%	-7.97%
32 DTSGX	+24.59%	+6.64%	-5.19%
33 TWCVX	+24.05%	+4.39%	-10.47%
34 JAVTX	+23.21%	+6.14%	-6.71%
35 SWSMX	+23.08%	+4.79%	-5.17%
36 TWCUX	+22.94%	+4.05%	-4.53%
37 SP-500	+22.59%	+2.72%	-0.88%
38 FMCPX	+21.57%	+4.77%	-4.82%
39 TWGTX	+20.28%	+13.72%	-10.06%
40 ALSCX	+19.49%	+3.05%	-8.61%
41 TAVFX	+16.69%	+3.48%	-1.57%
42 WAAEX	+16.50%	+1.02%	-9.40%
43 CWNOX	+16.39%	+7.68%	-4.42%
44 DTSVX	+16.22%	+1.59%	-0.93%
45 MERFX	+15.84%	+2.53%	+0.74%
46 FRSPX	+15.19%	+4.72%	-6.61%
47 STDIX	+14.65%	+2.49%	-6.84%
48 CREGX	+14.52%	+6.22%	-9.76%
49 FMGGX	+13.68%	+2.10%	-1.62%
50 RYPRX	+12.98%	+4.36%	-1.54%
51 JVBAX	+12.06%	+2.67%	-2.58%
52 EVLMX	+9.28%	+8.06%	-2.09%
53 RSVPX	+0.93%	+3.45%	-4.08%
54 HWSCX	N/A	+8.51%	-4.41%
55 VWMCX	N/A	+11.28%	-7.37%
56 WPVCX	N/A	+6.85%	-9.53%

	Since 06/21/95	*Since 03/21/96*	*Since 05/21/96*
57 WMICX	N/A	+8.14%	-3.92%
58 OAKSX	N/A	+13.74%	+0.32%
59 PASMX	N/A	+9.93%	-6.38%
60 JVMCX	N/A	+12.54%	-4.56%
61 VWEGX	N/A	+12.91%	-9.48%
62 JAOLX	N/A	+12.05%	-6.33%

After you have selected your fund based on its relative strength, you want to look at its moving average chart to see its current trend. Assuming it is positive, this fund would be a candidate for purchase. In the example, SteinRoe Capital Opportunities was still above its moving averages and had started back on an uptrend. The other two had not.

MOVING AVERAGES AND THE MARKET

We have looked at the Profitline Strategy as it relates to individual funds. It can also be used to analyze the entire market. Many technicians use the broad analysis to determine whether they should be in the market or in money markets. To use the strategy we need to select an index to apply our moving average against.

While the Dow Jones Industrial Averages is the most well known, I prefer to look at others. One index I like is the Dow Jones Composite. This index is made up of the Dow Jones Industrials, Transportation, and Utilities. This is preferred over the Dow Jones Industrials because it is broader-based, providing a wider look at the market. Additionally, you might also use the Standard & Poors 500 or the NASDAQ Index.

Figure 11-5 illustrates the use of the 39-week moving average for the Dow Jones Composite Index from 1993 to May 1996. Note the Buy (B) and Sell (S) points labeled on the chart. While there is no Buy/Sell whipsaw, the charts continued to provide a downside protection and once the market did take off, the moving averages kept you fully invested. Additionally, remember we are using no-load funds so even whipsaws don't cost transactions fees.

Figure 11-5 Dow Jones Composite

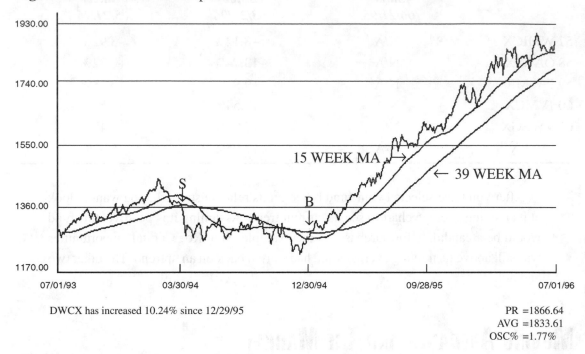

DWCX has increased 10.24% since 12/29/95

PR =1866.64
AVG =1833.61
OSC% =1.77%

Dollars & Sense: Use moving average comparisons and broad market indices to give a strong indication of the current market direction.

Following the moving average of the market is an excellent way of determining whether to be in or out of the market. For example, if you know the Dow Composite is running above its short- and long-term moving average, you could feel very comfortable about being in the market. If, on the other hand, the Dow Composite had crossed its 39-week average trending down and your selected fund had just crossed its short-term moving average, prudence would suggest selling your fund would be a safe bet.

Upgrading Your Funds

Even though the market is performing well (above 39-week moving average) and your fund is moving well (above 39-week moving average), your fund's RSM may be reducing and other potential fund selections growing at a faster rate. You know this because you should be reviewing the fund's RSM on a monthly basis. If this occurs, you may want to consider upgrading by moving from your slower performing fund to the better performing one. To make upgrading profitable, you should be in a no-load environment and it is best if the move has no transaction cost. Additionally, you may want to move in increments by perhaps moving $1/2$ of your position now and the balance in a week if conditions stay the same. By using the upgrading technique, you can always try to maintain at least part of your money in the highest RSM fund.

Table 11-2 Comparing Upgrade Candidates			
FUND	*1-Year Return*	*90-Day Return*	*30-Day Return*
Alger Capital Appreciation	70.23%	13.18%	4.45%
American Heritage	19.05	7.14	0.00
Bull & Bear Special Equity	46.47	14.06	6.66
Crabbe Huson Special	6.31	1.19	1.16
Founders Special	24.98	9.62	0.75
FundManager Aggressive Growth	25.66	9.23	4.57
INVESCO Dynamics	37.52	6.39	2.24
Janus Olympus	NA	19.09	4.03
Markman Aggressive Growth	NA	8.43	4.65
Permanent Portfolio Aggressive Growth	23.04	2.70	1.86
Rydex Series Trust Nova	36.34	3.83	7.44
SteinRoe Capital Opportunities	82.40	21.56	7.98
Strong Discovery	27.16	8.54	4.80
20th Century Ultra	36.54	7.51	5.52
Value Line Special Situations	29.05	5.49	1.61
Warburg Pincus Post Venture Capital	NA	16.75	4.72
Wasatch Aggressive Equity	29.13	12.17	2.05
Citizens Emerging Growth	55.62	15.83	7.11

Which fund would you choose? See the end of the chapter for your answer.

THE THREE BIGGEST ADVANTAGES OF THE PROFITLINE STRATEGY

1. It allows you to stay in the market as long as the uptrend continues, thus taking advantage of sustained rising markets with no guesswork.

2. It removes you from the market when a downtrend has started to protect profits you have previously made.

3. It gives you a reliable method to select the top-performing stock, bond, or mutual fund in any market.

LET'S REMEMBER THIS:

▶ Use 39-week moving averages as a buy/sell indicator to increase your return.

▶ Moving averages can be used to make general market decisions and individual fund purchases.

▶ The Profitline Strategy combines moving averages with relative strength to create a powerful investment tool.

Table 11-2 ANSWER: I would pick SteinRoe Capital Opportunities in the upgrade question. There is certainly nothing wrong with Alger Capital Appreciation, but I particularly like the fact that SteinRoe's current RSM is stronger.

▼

How to Invest in Sector Funds for Big Returns

What We Are Going to Talk About in This Chapter:

- ▶ How You Can Use Specialized Knowledge to Boost Your Returns
- ▶ Where to Find the Best Selection of Sector Funds
- ▶ The Secrets to Selecting the Best Sector Funds

In some respects, life just keeps improving for mutual fund investors. Perhaps the most significant advancement may be found in the growing number of funds and the rapidly increasing areas of specialization. For those of us long familiar with the securities industry, we can remember a time when mutual funds were regarded as little more than a curiosity, something new that didn't have a good enough track record to be invested in. Times have certainly changed. Now there are more mutual funds than there are stocks on the New York Stock Exchange.

In general, every type of security is accessible as a mutual fund: money markets, bonds, options, preferred stocks, and common stocks. Through market indexes you can invest in the entire market or certain sections of the market. More specifically, mutual funds can be found in many different forms, depending upon your particular investment objective. For more conservatively-minded investors, index funds and balanced funds may suit your purpose. If you are willing to accept a higher level of risk in return for higher potential rewards, there are more aggressive options. One such option is a sector fund.

Perhaps you've heard the term sector fund before and wondered just what type of mutual fund that is supposed to be. Maybe you've actually invested in a type of sector fund without even realizing it. Whatever your introduction, sector fund investing should be considered as an option of your overall mutual fund strategy.

The word "sector" refers to a portion of something. With respect to mutual funds, "sector" refers to any particular industry. Thus, a sector fund is a type of mutual fund whose portfolio of stocks is made up of companies in the same industry. Health care funds, technology funds, utilities funds, and leisure funds are just a few of the categories of sector funds available to investors. In general, any type of fund that relates the name of the representative industry in the title of the fund can reasonably be assumed to be a sector fund.

The Fidelity family of mutual funds offers the greatest selection of sector funds for investment (see Table 12-1). Other fund families, both load and no-load, offer at least one or two sector funds for investment.

Table 12-1 Fidelity Sector Funds

FIDELITY SELECT PORTFOLIOS

Air Transportation	Electronics	Money Market
American Gold	Energy	Multimedia
Automotive	Energy Service	Natural Gas
Biotechnology	Environmental Services	Paper & Forest Products
Brokerage & Investment Management	Financial Services	Precious Metals & Minerals
Chemicals	Food & Agriculture	Regional Banks
Computers	Health Care	Retailing
Construction & Housing	Home Finance	Software & Computer Services
Consumer Products	Industrial Materials	Technology
Defense & Aerospace	Insurance	Telecommunications
Developing Communications	Leisure	Transportation
	Medical Delivery	Utilities Growth

The most common concern voiced regarding sector funds is that they decrease a fund's diversity. The fund's diversity was one of its major advantages in the first place. Rather than possessing a portfolio of 50–75 different stocks representing a number of different industries (a "typical" mutual fund), a sector fund portfolio is usually composed of 20–30 individual issues, all from the same industry. You have diversity of individual stocks, but they are all related to the same industry.

How can you use this investment vehicle to your advantage? Let's say that you were quite confident about the prospects of the biotechnology sector in the near future. To take advantage of this impending "boom," you may decide to purchase shares of stock from one of the more popular companies representing this industry, such as Amgen. Would this be the best way to capitalize on the growth of an entire industry? Probably not. By selecting one particular company, you are risking as much on the performance of that one company as you are on the performance of the industry it represents. When you invest in a biotechnology sector fund, however, you are poised to take advantage of that industry's growth without having the risk that one particular company may succeed.

Dollars & Sense: Use sector funds to take advantage of specialized information you may have about an industry. A computer consultant may learn how to make more money on his investments by investing in the computer, software, and technology sector.

Although the sector fund can be very appropriate for the investor who has specialized information, if you don't have such information, you must understand that you are increasing your risk by specializing. Because they are specific to an industry, sector funds tend to be very volatile. The reason is that you have lost the diversity of spreading your investment across a broad market. If you are a conservative investor, and aren't used to very large price swings, then you can quickly become uncomfortable using sector funds.

For conservative investors who simply must try sector funds, I would suggest doing so in limited amounts. In the beginning, I recommend only 5%–10% of your overall portfolio. Few investors should ever have more than 40% of their portfolio tied up in sector funds and 15%–30% is a more realistic figure.

Investors who like to characterize themselves as "very aggressive" sometimes make the mistake of placing all of their investment monies with sector funds. This is very aggressive for mutual fund investing and should only be done by active investors willing to closely watch the performance of their fund. Industries that may enjoy rapid, short-term growth stages may not see such growth again for several years. Perhaps the most notable example of this predicament may be found within the technology industry. The years 1982 and 1983 were quite favorable to technology stocks (and the mutual fund portfolios containing them). For the remainder of the '80s, the technology industry was a "dog," and many investors who placed a great deal of money in technology-based funds in late 1983 and after were quite disappointed year after year. In the '90s we have seen a similar pattern as it relates to technology. Good years will be followed by weak or bad years. Consequently, investors should be prepared to keep close watch on their sector funds and limit the percentage in their portfolio unless they are very aggressive.

Figure 12-2   The Highs & Lows of Sector Investing   While you can make a lot of money investing in sectors, you can also lose a great deal. The charts below illustrate the difference between Fidelity Select Electronics and Fidelity Select Precious Metals during 1995. If you had invested in Fidelity Select Precious Metals, you would have yielded -3.34%, on the other hand, Fidelity Select Electronics would have yielded +69.40%.

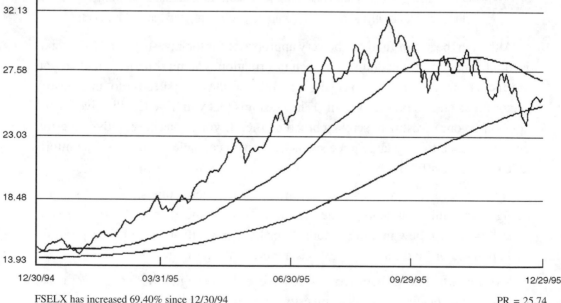

Fidelity Select Electronics

FSELX has increased 69.40% since 12/30/94

PR = 25.74
AVG = 27.03
OSC% = -5.02%

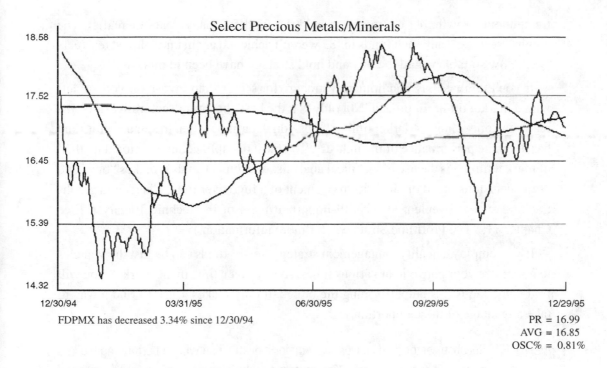

Select Precious Metals/Minerals

FDPMX has decreased 3.34% since 12/30/94

PR = 16.99
AVG = 16.85
OSC% = 0.81%

CAN YOU MANAGE SECTOR FUNDS?

While a number of different types of management strategies seemed to have gained favor on behalf of mutual fund portfolios, you can actually divide them into two broad categories: buy and hold, and market timing. As I've suggested throughout this book, I've never been a big fan of the buy and hold strategy because it promotes investing with blinders on to everything that is going on around you. I not only think it is impractical for most people, I don't even think it's the best for those who follow it. For sector fund investors, I am even less enamored with the approach. The buy and hold strategy states that by selecting a couple of funds with quality track records and holding them for years, your eventual return will more than justify the market fluctuations you will encounter along the way. If you follow this strategy, the funds selected for buy and hold should be well-diversified funds across many industries with better-than-average track records. Sector funds just wouldn't work very well in this case.

Consider the technology example again. You would have been very disappointed if you purchased a technology fund in '82 and realized some of that industry's tremendous growth, but continued to hold the fund for many years thereafter. The "highs" seen by many such funds in '83 weren't achieved again until almost ten years later. How suitable would the buy and hold strategy have been in this case?

If you eliminate buy and hold as a strategy for sector fund investing, you are left with a market timing approach. Not only is it the best choice for sector investors, it's really the only choice. Market timing helps you determine when to sell a sector fund based on the performance of the industry. The most disciplined, unemotional method of market timing is the use of technical analysis. A technical analyst makes "buy" and "sell" decisions based on the price movement of a fund over time. Charts and graphs tracking such movement are the all-important tools of the technical analyst. (See Chapter 11, "The Profitline Strategy," for more information.)

If you employ a quality management strategy, sector funds can be just the vehicles to maximize your portfolio at various times. At any given time in the market, you will find some industries outperforming the others. It only makes sense to find a way to take advantage of these opportunities.

Dollars & $ense: Because sector funds cover every major industry, one will be performing well no matter what the economy. Use sectors to take advantage of your knowledge of economic shifts.

History of Sector Funds

Although sector funds have only recently become popular, the very first sector fund came into existence in 1928. This fund specialized in the financial services sector, and you can still buy shares of it today. It is the Century Shares Trust, and its portfolio is made up predominantly of stocks representing the banking and insurance industries. Remember, though, that this industry (like all industries) moves in a rather cyclical pattern. If you were to review this fund's annual performance over the course of its existence, you would find that some time periods exhibited outstanding results and others were no good. To demonstrate how the temperamental cycles turn, let's look at a couple of sample periods. For Century Shares Trust, the years 1958–1961 witnessed an average annual return of 28.5% (but not one of those years witnessed a return in the 10–20% range). Conversely, the years 1964–1967 saw the average annual return sit at the -7.3% mark! This should tell you that while sector fund positions can cause difficulties if you're not paying attention, they can also prove to be invaluable wealth-building tools.

How to Pick Your Sector Fund

Sector funds are generally selected through the use of either one of two methods: fundamental analysis or technical analysis. Some stock pickers even use a combination of the two methods. Let's look at them more closely.

Fundamental analysis is the process of selecting securities for investment by examining the "fundamentals" of a business or industry. The fundamental analyst is attempting to determine the prospects of a stock by examining its earnings relative to its market price. If a stock is sufficiently under-valued, it may be ripe for investment. If the stock is over-valued, the fundamental analyst will probably pass it up. While the very nature of fundamental analysis makes it more conducive to individual stock selection as opposed to mutual funds containing 20–100 different companies, the broader fundamental measures can be used to evaluate sector funds.

Money Talks: Fundamental analysis of a company involves focusing on the performance of a company's sales earnings and profits, their relationship to each other, and their relationship to the price of the stock in the company.

Fundamental analysis involves the examination of company indicators, industry indicators, and national economic indicators. It is these industry and national economic indicators that you will pay the most attention to in sector fundamental analysis. One area of concentration would be the current business cycle. Targeting the movement of interest rates with the economy is an example of fundamental analysis.

Another example of important economic information is the "leading" indicators of the business cycle: housing starts and durable goods orders. Earlier we looked at consumer and producer price indexes along with the nation's unemployment figures. All of these numbers help fundamental analysis of a sector. By comparing the current economy to other economic cycles, you can see which industries performed best in the past in similar economic environments.

Technical analysis, on the other hand, does not concern itself with the "fundamentals" of a company or industry (see Chapter 11, "The Profitline Strategy"). As a matter of fact, this type of analysis cares little for economic indicators such as interest rates or housing starts. A technical analyst cares only about the price movement of a particular security, movement that is tracked through the use of charts and graphs. A technical analyst, specifically a "chartist," will review the historical movement of the price of a security and make buy and sell decisions based on that movement.

Money Talks: Technical analysis is the study of the price patterns of a company's stock and its relationship to the market.

There are variations within the spectrum of technical analysis that allow some flexibility to how the historical data is to be measured and utilized. A method of technical analysis that I have found to be the most reliable is one that uses a tool known as "moving averages." As discussed in the chapter on Profitline Strategy, a moving average refers to the average price of a stock, bond, or mutual fund over a designated period of time. The average "moves" because it is ongoing. For example, if you use the familiar 39-week moving average, you will be recalculating the current average price of the fund at the end of each week. As you include the latest price, the oldest one is dropped from consideration. This average price is then compared to the current actual price of the given fund. Depending on the relation between the fund's current price and its moving average, a decision to buy or sell may be made. (See Chapter 11, "The Profitline Strategy," for a complete explanation of moving averages.)

The implementation of technical analysis isn't quite that simple, but you now have some idea of what both technical and fundamental analysis are all about. This discussion is significant because it highlights for you the two best methods to use in selection of your sector fund. While I am a strong believer in technical analysis, I believe that the incorporation of fundamental analysis can complement a chartist's strategies. For example, the use of interest rates to determine which type of vehicle (stocks, bonds, or money markets) is most appropriate at a point in time is a form of broad-based fundamental analysis. Using this information and applying it to a particular economy might show you that interest rates are falling. Using this knowledge you then use technical analysis to find the best performing stocks, bonds, internationals, sectors, or other areas of investment alternatives.

Dollars & Sense: To select the best performing funds use the information available from both technical and fundamental indicators.

MAKING THE MOVE

Most quality fund families have at least one fund that targets a specific industry. However, some families have resisted the trend for a variety of reasons. If, after reading this chapter, you feel that you would like to invest, you will have many options.

If you anticipate being a very active trader of mutual fund shares, you may want to consider opening a brokerage account with a notable discount broker, which was discussed in Chapter 4. These accounts will provide you with greater selection and opportunities. Another option available to you is to maintain your base or primary mutual fund account(s) with one of your favorite families, and to then select your sector fund (those not offered by your family) from the other families available. The final choice for you is to simply open or switch your no-load mutual fund account with a fund family that offers you the sector funds that interest you.

Dollars & Sense: The two best ways to set up an account for sector fund investing is through either a discount broker or a large fund family with a wide range of mutual fund selections.

To assist you in beginning your sector fund investing, I have included a number of fund family choices that are consistent with my belief that your mutual fund accounts need only be located at high-quality, versatile, no-low or low-load fund families.

Fidelity Investments
82 Devonshire Street
Boston, MA 02109
1-800-544-6666

Fidelity mutual funds are legendary for both their tremendous selections and overall performance. This fund family possesses the highest number of sector fund choices available anywhere. You will almost always find a Fidelity sector fund ranked as one of the best performing funds at any given time. Likewise, you will almost always find one of Fidelity's sector funds ranked the lowest of all sector funds (but you won't likely hear about it).

Known as "select" funds, Fidelity sector funds assess a 3% load on the front-end and a 1% load on the back-end sale. However, they offer the most comprehensive selection and allow you to switch between sectors (with limitations) without incurring additional fees. This fund family is ideal for an active sector investor. (You may wish to refer to Table 12-1 to see the sector alternatives offered by Fidelity.)

Invesco Funds
P.O. Box 2040
Denver, CO 80201
1-800-525-8085

Next to Fidelity, the Invesco Funds mutual fund family offers the greatest number of sector choices. The beauty of families such as Fidelity and Invesco is that they present a solid range of diversified funds in addition to their sector offerings, enabling investors to contain their total fund activity within a single family. Additionally, the Invesco Funds family is committed to the no-load philosophy with respect to all of their funds, and the low minimum investment requirements provide for easy access by all investors. Here is a list of the eight sector funds, called "strategic portfolios," available at Invesco:

Invesco Strategic Energy

Invesco Strategic Environmental Services

Invesco Strategic Financial Services

Invesco Strategic Gold

Invesco Strategic Health Services

Invesco Strategic Leisure

Invesco Strategic Technology

Invesco Strategic Utilities

T. Rowe Price
100 E. Pratt Street
Baltimore, MD 21202
1-800-638-5660

T. Rowe Price mutual funds offer a solid array of diversified growth funds for more aggressive investors. Even so, their sector offerings are limited to just one: T. Rowe Price Science and Technology. It's sort of a hybrid offering, naming industries general enough in its title to provide the fund manager with a great deal of flexibility. Price funds are completely no-load.

Please understand that these specific examples of funds should not be regarded as recommendations. The volatility of sector mutual funds demands that you keep a watchful eye on their performance, both prior to and during your actual investment. Remember that sector funds should never be regarded as complete portfolios unto themselves, and your broad-based, long-term investment objectives should always be considered when selecting any mutual fund. You will find, however, that the tremendous potential offered by these funds is tough to overlook, and their incorporation in your portfolio through the use of a solid strategy will help to make your overall fund performance a consistent winner.

Let's Remember This:

- ► Sector funds offer a unique alternative to regular mutual fund investing.

- ► Sector funds can be used to target strengths in the economy.

- ► Technical analysis is a successful technique for monitoring the performance of sector funds.

▼

Strategies For the Aggressive Investor

What We Are Going to Talk About in This Chapter:

▶ Buying Mutual Funds on Margin Increases Your Investing Leverage

▶ How to Increase Returns by Specializing

▶ How to Spot Fast-moving Funds

Very little is written today for the aggressive investor. Most books are designed for mainstream readers and the word aggressive isn't usually part of their vocabulary. If you're not aggressive, skip this chapter. There is no sense adding worry to your investment process. For those of you who do tend to be more aggressive, this chapter is for you.

First, let me review that there is always a risk/reward ratio to making an investment. Don't tell me that you want to be more aggressive, but on the other hand that you can't afford to lose principal. These are mutually exclusive concepts and the sooner you admit it the better investor you'll be. Remember, I'm the guy that believes the most important thing an investor should know is who you are both mentally and financially.

Second, let me point out that you don't have to be 100% conservative or 100% aggressive. Somewhere between the two may very well be a happy medium. For example, part of your investment dollars, 10%–15% for example, could be set up in a separate account to be used more aggressively. Doing this may make you feel bolder, it may protect the other 85%–90% of your nest egg, or it may be done for educational value. Whatever the reason, setting aside some money in a special account for aggressive investing gives you an added element of diversification and that in itself is a sound idea. In fact, modern portfolio theory and the prudent investment rule are now both acknowledging that at least a small portion of your portfolio might want to be placed in a more aggressive (I didn't say speculative) posture.

USE SPECIAL SKILLS TO INCREASE YOUR RETURNS

One way to increase your aggressiveness in mutual fund investing is to become a specialist. A specialist narrows down the plethora of mutual funds to a handful of funds all in a narrow range of a specialty.

For example, you might read the chapter on sector investing and decide that sectors offer a unique opportunity for high profits. You could reduce your mutual fund investing to the sector market, research each fund available, chart the fund in the sector marketplace and be an active trader. As a specialist trader you would always be working with Relative Strength Momentum (RSM) rankings and buying and selling funds based upon current performance. This kind of trading can enable you to find big run-ups of 60% or more. On the other hand, you could lose with a fund's down turn, which is precisely why it is called an aggressive strategy.

Money Talks: Relative Strength Momentum (RSM) is a comparison between a specific fund, the general market, and all other funds of its type. The higher its RSM, the faster its price is moving compared to the others.

Another example of a specialist would be someone who deals only in international funds or perhaps, and even more aggressive, only in emerging country funds. These funds, like sectors, can offer big rewards but carry big risks. To take advantage of them, the specialist concentrates on this specific area and learns to understand the pattern of fluctuation. Using this knowledge you would be able to spot trends before the general investor and take advantage of unique price fluctuations that occur in these specialized fields.

In addition to becoming a specialist, you can also increase the aggressiveness of your account by the manner in which you hold it. This can be done either by margin investing or by shorting mutual funds.

MARGIN INVESTING

Once you feel you can consistently earn high returns, then you can increase those yields by buying on margin (loan). A margin account is a special account set up by a brokerage firm to loan you money using your securities, in this case mutual funds, as security for the loan. Under the current stock exchange rules you can borrow money up to 50% of the value of your mutual funds. If your funds increase in value, then you can continue to borrow more money. However, if your funds decrease in value, then you must add more money to the account to stay within the lending ratio (50%). If your account drops below the ratio you will get a telephone call from your broker asking you to put more money into the account. This is referred to as a "margin call." If you are unable or unwilling to add additional money to your account, then the broker is required to sell enough of the securities held in the account to return it back to the proper ratio.

For all their apparent complications, margin accounts are really quite simple. The broker offers an interest rate (adjustable). If you can make a better return by investing than the cost of money you are paying, you get to keep the spread. You have made money on other people's money. On the other hand, if you lose money based on your investment selections, you will not only have to pay that amount back to the brokerage firm but you will also have to pay the interest on the borrowed money as well. In a down market you can lose a lot of money very fast. As a general rule, only consider buying on margin when the general market trend is good.

Dollars & Sense: Margin interest is deductible as interest used for investments. This advantage lowers your real cost of the transaction by the amount of your marginal tax bracket.

SHORTING MUTUAL FUNDS

Although not a common practice, it is possible to sell mutual funds short. This means that you will be selling mutual funds that you don't own in the hopes that the fund will decline and you will be able to buy funds at a future date to cover (replace) the funds you sold. Obviously, the time to use this strategy is when you feel that a fund is falling in value.

Money Talks: "Selling short" means selling mutual funds that you don't own but have temporarily borrowed from a brokerage firm. You gain a profit if you can replace them by buying shares in the same fund at a lower price.

The discount brokerage firm of Fidelity Investments and the discount brokerage firm Jack White and Co. are two firms that offer mutual fund shorting. Through special accounts they have established, the firm will loan you shares of a particular fund on a margin basis. These shares are then sold at market to meet your short sale. The cash generated from the sale is held in your account as collateral for the borrowed shares. At a date in the future, you purchase the same fund shares in the open market and use them to replace the borrowed shares. The broker then releases your cash being held as collateral. If you were able to buy the shares at a price lower than you paid for the borrowed shares, then you get to keep the profit. If your purchase resulted in a deficiency then you will receive a margin call to make up the difference in cash.

Selling mutual funds short could also technically be used as a hedge. If you like a fund long-term, but have concerns for it over the short term, then you could place a short sale on the mutual funds you hold. If the fund does go down, then you will have protected your position.

Adding greater risk to your investing is not for everyone. However, it can be exciting and profitable if you are willing to spend the time needed to understand the approach and how to protect your downside.

Let's Remember This:

▶ There is a time and place for aggressive investing. Just make sure it fits your goals and objectives.

▶ Selling mutual funds short is an aggressive strategy that can be used successfully by contrarian investors.

▶ Increasing your aggressiveness in investing means you will also be increasing your risk. Make sure that stance fits your goals and objectives.

▼

How to Take Advantage of the Global Economy

What We Are Going to Talk About in This Chapter:

► Why You Should Consider Investing Internationally

► How Emerging Nations Offer a Unique Opportunity to the Mutual Fund Investor

► The Risk and Rewards of International Investing

This chapter is your guide to an area of mutual fund investing unfamiliar to many investors: international or global mutual funds. While interest in this area of investing has increased dramatically in recent years, many investors don't understand foreign investing. Even relatively sophisticated investors are frequently unfamiliar with all the ramifications and various types of risks inherent in such funds.

I once had a discussion with a potential client who had his IRA invested solely in the international fund of a particular, well-known fund family. The fund was a load fund and the salesman reportedly told him that the opportunities were much better overseas. Time was of the essence, the salesman told him, to make a move. If he waited, he would miss out on the impending "boom" in the overseas market. Was the salesman right? The pitch sounded good to the novice fund investor.

That, of course, is the problem. What this investor received was a pitch, not an objective piece of information. Because the securities industry is so heavily commission-driven, the best interests of the client can be forgotten. As it turns out, this individual has spent the last several years in a fund that has, with the ups and downs frequently found in the equity arena, returned about the same as a passbook savings account. There are many new opportunities that have opened up for investors to buy in overseas markets. Unfortunately, because of the intrigue of the international markets they can be romanced to trap the unwary. This chapter will help you see through that trap and understand the true advantages and disadvantages.

Why Invest Internationally, and Why Do It With Mutual Funds?

With the numerous opportunities for mutual fund investment available in the United States, why consider investing outside the country? Is it absolutely necessary to invest internationally to achieve a solid level of growth from your invested monies? The answer is that investing outside the U.S. is not a necessity, but an opportunity. If you understand overseas investing, you will have other opportunities available when the U.S. market turns down. Frequently, the markets do not run parallel and the use of international markets offers another form of diversification for your accounts. When the U.S. market becomes difficult you can simply focus in a different direction.

Are there times when investing in a broad-based international stock fund is not so good? Certainly, just as there are times when it can be highly profitable. You'll see, however, that it is no different from the investment discussion for any type of domestic fund in which you might invest, be it an index, aggressive growth, or sector fund. In this sense, foreign funds are like any others. However, there are some key points to consider that differentiate international and U.S. based funds, and that can make international fund investing a very exciting proposition.

Dollars & $ense: Use international funds to add an additional type of diversification to your investment portfolio and to provide alternatives when the U.S. markets are down.

First of all, a large number of all the world's Blue Chip companies are located outside the United States. This simple fact alone is enough to consider investing in an international fund. Additionally, the fastest growing area of new opportunities for investment are located in foreign markets. Consequently, as our economy becomes more global in nature these new opportunities create possibilities for profits that can only come from rapidly expanding economies.

Second, and perhaps most important, various regions of the world that have been virtually inaccessible to U.S. investors (and investment, period) are experiencing exciting changes that should bode well for international investment in the years ahead. The first region that comes to mind is the Commonwealth of Independent States (formerly the Soviet Union), and other eastern European regions. There is a strong push for economic reform in these areas, and this reform is going to be in the image of capitalism, or a free market system. There has always been tremendous demand for many goods and services (some very basic) in these regions, but the restrictive and inefficient economic policies of those countries have not come close to satisfying the demand. The free market systems will, of course, stimulate competition to meet this demand in the coming years. Additionally, the countries of the Far East represent some of the most formidable economies anywhere. Although many analysts predicted that Japan's growth would slow, there are other Pacific Rim and Southeast Asian countries that may make this region of the world ideal for investments for many years. In fact, the greatest international opportunities are those presented by the so-called emerging markets, and many of these markets emanate from this region. The same holds true for many Latin American countries. This part of the world will represent substantial opportunity for foreign investment.

Dollars & Sense: Emerging nations offer unusual opportunities not available in developed countries. While the growth opportunities are big, remember that additional rewards are always associated with added risk.

Although you can see why foreign markets are so promising and so appropriate for at least a small portion of your investment portfolio, you must find the most reasonable way to take advantage of these markets. Even if you haven't invested in mutual funds before, you will quickly see why they are the most realistic option to invest in foreign markets. While both fund investors and stock investors may share some of the same risks, the stock investor will encounter additional problems. First, the normally simple act of purchasing shares of stock is not so simple outside the U.S. You must consider the restraints on timely trading by basic time zone differences. Several markets are closing down about the time most United States brokers are at work and placing orders. That same U.S. broker is going to have to be able to get you a price quote on the particular issue of interest. It can take many hours before foreign market quotes are received. The very fact that your broker has to deal with a foreign broker can increase the logistical difficulties. If that's not enough, some countries prohibit direct investment from foreigners. Unfortunately, many of the nations that prohibit direct stock investment are the ones that offer the greatest potential. Korea is an excellent example of an emerging market nation that disallows such investment. Is there a recourse? Yes there is. It's called a single-country, closed-end mutual fund and I'll cover that a little later.

Another problem for stock investors is the transactional problem of trade settlement overseas. In the United States, when a trade is executed in an individual security, the buyer must make payment in three business days following the trade date. This date for payment is known as the settlement date. There is no such hard-and-fast rule in foreign markets. Trades in such markets can take several weeks to settle. Italy has an interesting rule requiring the physical delivery of the purchased securities in order to settle. Of course, this creates a liquidity problem and would make life quite rough on active traders.

While the risks mentioned may seem a bit overwhelming to an individual investor, the mutual fund manager is experienced in these problems and they have no effect on the international mutual fund investor. In this case, the management fee you are paying is for more than just picking the right companies to invest in.

The Risk of International Mutual Fund Investing

The subject of risk as it pertains to international mutual funds can become somewhat involved. Are funds made up of foreign securities riskier than domestic funds? Some financial advisors believe they are quite risky, while others will tell you their global diversification helps investors reduce their overall investment risk. The fact is, international funds come in all shapes and sizes, from conservative to highly aggressive. Your job is to determine your own objectives and match it with the goals of the fund. Additionally, you will need to be aware to some extent of the economic and political climate of the area of the world in which you are investing. Political stability around the globe is a different situation than we are accustomed to in the United States.

Currency risk is the most significant type of risk found by international investors. The constant fluctuations between the U.S. dollar and the world's various currencies make this risk element the most closely monitored. The reason is because international funds will contain foreign securities that are based around the currency of the country or region in which you are investing. Those securities are denominated in the currency of the respective homelands. It is not enough to consider the change in the price of the security. You must also monitor the exchange rates between the U.S. dollar and foreign currencies. Here is a simple example: Let's suppose you won a British stock, and its value rises from 100 pounds per share to 125 per share. You've gained 25% on your investment, you're happy with that, and you want to sell. Now, here's where currency risk comes into play. Let's suppose that when you purchased the British stock, one U.S. dollar was equal to four British pounds. Now, when you sell, the U.S. dollar is equal to six British pounds. The value of the British pound was weakened against the dollar. How much has it weakened? By two pounds, or 50%! So, when you sell your British stock, which has appreciated 25% in share price, but convert back to the U.S. dollar, against which the pound dropped 50% during that time, you actually lost 25% in the deal. So remember, the value of a foreign security in U.S. dollars will increase when the dollar weakens, or loses value, against the given security's currency. Conversely, the value of the same security in U.S. dollars will decrease (as we saw in our example) when the dollar strengthens, or gains value, against the security's currency. That is the basic idea, but things can become even more complicated for the international fund manager (and, in turn, you). The actual act of converting currencies to purchase foreign securities can involve various expenses. Currency exchange is highly regulated, and there can be exchange controls and restrictions that may adversely affect the value of the fund's assets.

Is there anything the mutual fund manager can do to at least alleviate some of the risk associated with adverse movements in currency exchange rates? Yes, by hedging. This strategy involves the use of a forward currency exchange contract. The contract enables the mutual fund to buy or sell a specific foreign security at a set date and price. The fund manager can use such contracts for a specific security, or with all positions in general. The fund manager has the ability to actually hold fast the exchange rate between trade dates and settlement dates, thereby reducing some of the volatility.

Dollars & Sense:

Three added risks of international investing are:

1. Currency risk;
2. Lower government control over international public companies; and
3. Economic and political changes are less stable than in the United States.

Another one of the potential downsides of investing in foreign companies is that, in general, they are not subject to the regulatory controls placed on U.S. issuers. The accessibility of public information about foreign companies is limited enough for nationals, let alone for foreigners. For example, accounting and other financial reporting procedures are no where near as stringent as with United States companies. While the increased emphasis on business regulation in this country is welcomed by prospective investors, those same investors will find a very different story in foreign countries.

The lack of regulation of corporations that issue securities is also a factor with the foreign exchange and brokerage process itself. Again, citizens of the Unites States have the benefit of knowing that there is an increasingly strict level of compliance that must be met by all of the principals involved in the securities industry here. In this country, the Code of Arbitration procedure has proven to be a cost-effective and expedient method of resolving disputes between customers and brokerages, traders, etc. Similar protections are, in general, unavailable to investors dealing with foreign exchanges and traders. Another aspect to this "market risk" is the fact that many markets, like the smaller, emerging markets, will have a much smaller amount of market activity (i.e., volume of trading) than is found here. This lower level of activity can make the securities traded on these exchanges more difficult to buy and consequently, more difficult to sell. The inherent volatility and loss of liquidity with such issues makes the process much riskier. And there is one more thing to remember. Unlike the United States, which allows for more freedom in bartering over the brokerage commission to be charged, foreign brokerages usually have set prices for the cost of the transactions, and those prices are quite often higher than what may be found in the U.S.

Taxation is also sometimes a problem in foreign countries. Non-residents are usually assessed special withholding taxes by the particular foreign government, which will mean lower dividends paid to shareholders. This issue can become especially significant if you need income from your investment.

Besides currency risk, I guess the type of risk that is the most significant for you as an international investor is the risk associated with political and economic changes. Because your biggest potential gains come from investing in a company before it reaches its primary growth stage, this may mean purchasing the securities of a country whose entire market condition is relatively new and in flux. Third World or Latin American countries, many of which have been in depression status for years, are now beginning to show signs of life. However, the political upheaval that is so common in these regions means that the futures of any companies or entire markets can be uncertain, at best. An excellent example of this uncertainty can be found in the Guangdong Province, located in southern China near Hong Kong. By all accounts, this is one of the fastest growing areas in the world economically, a unique region of mainland China where capitalism has been allowed to flourish, in spite of the official policies of the country. A number of Hong Kong-based businesses have set up factories and plants in this area (the formidable China Light and Power is one). However, because of the precarious futures awaiting both mainland China and Hong Kong, any investment activities in this region warrant close attention. Southeast Asian countries, and Latin-American countries like Mexico, are other excellent examples of nations whose investment potential is considered excellent for the long term, but whose economic architecture must be observed closely.

Is that enough risk for you? As you can clearly see, the international fund investor has a great deal to consider. You may be wondering if the rewards are worth the risks. The fact is, international investing can be highly profitable and, as I have mentioned, an excellent alternative for you to have available. Additionally, because you are using mutual funds, the risks we have discussed are handled by professional managers and that is what you are paying them for.

TERMINOLOGY: "GLOBAL," "INTERNATIONAL," AND "COUNTRY" FUNDS

Frequently, you may hear the terms "global fund" and "international fund" used interchangeably. I will even use them that way for generalization. Nevertheless, there is a difference between these two types of funds. From some fund families you will have the opportunity to purchase both types of funds, so it is important that you know and understand the difference.

A *global fund* is made up of both U.S. and foreign securities, while an *international fund* consists of only foreign securities. However, these definitions are not standardized, so things are not quite that simple. In fact, many international funds actually have U.S. securities in their portfolios. A more realistic definition of an international fund would have at least two-thirds of the fund's portfolio invested in foreign securities, while leaving a sizable chunk of the portfolio for investment in American companies. A good definition of a global fund says that at least 25% of the fund's portfolio is invested in foreign securities. The 25% requirement really is not a lot, and you need to be aware that some so-called "global" funds are really not so global. Without knowing it, you may be purchasing shares of a domestic mutual fund that has a few foreign companies in its portfolio. Again, this is where you need to pay attention, know what it is you are buying, and read the prospectuses carefully to see how the portfolio is made up. International and global mutual funds may diversify across several markets, or may target specific regions of the world, and will do so in varying percentages.

In addition to global and international funds, there are other funds known as country funds. *Country funds* are mutual funds that are made up of the securities of one particular nation. While these types of funds are available as both open-end and closed-end funds, it is the closed-end funds that have some of the highest growth potentials. A good example of an open-end country fund would be any of the various "Japan Funds" offered by many of the well-known fund families. Investments in country funds are generally considered to be the most volatile types of foreign fund investments, as they are not diversified across several markets. The country funds that represent smaller, emerging market nations (Korea, for example) are easily the most volatile of funds.

The Vehicles: Money Market, Bond, and Stock Funds

Keeping in mind all we have discussed so far, it is now time to turn to a discussion of the actual mutual fund vehicles that we will utilize to augment and strengthen our portfolio, when it is appropriate. Remember, international funds are no different from domestic funds, in that there are both winners and losers. Which of these categories you invest in will depend on timeliness of investment in the specific geographical regions, your personal investment objectives, mutual fund investment strategies, etc.

Money markets with foreign securities in the portfolios represent the safest way to invest internationally. At times you can use these funds to increase your yield over U.S. money markets. Remember, however, that times will change and you must continually watch for currency price changes and compare the international fund return to your U.S. account. If you're going to be in a money market, find one with some global diversification.

Both Chapter 10, "How The Economy and Interest Rates Effect Your Mutual Fund Return," and Chapter 11, "The Profitline Strategy," discussed the fact that interest rate changes effect both prices. When interest rates rise, bond values drop. If you own an 8% bond, and interest rates rise past 8% to say, 10%, the 8% bond loses value. The 10% bond is the higher yielding security, and is more desirable. To compensate, if you wanted to sell the 8% bond, you would have to sell at a discounted price. Conversely, when interest rates fall, bond values rise. That same 8% bond—should interest rates fall below 8% to 6%—is now the higher yielding bond, and becomes more valuable.

It is the role of the international bond fund manager to keep a close eye on the interest rates of countries around the world. The international bond fund manager must have a thorough knowledge of world economics; specifically, the fund manager must be astute at identifying nations whose interest rates are at "highs" and where reverse inflation or disinflation, is in progress. Disinflation results from a "tightening" of the money supply. Such a tightening brings on falling prices, as well as falling interest rates. Inflation has a negative influence on bond instruments for two reasons. First, inflation causes interest rates to rise, which weakens bond values. Second, and equally as problematic for some, inflation causes the current income that some investors depend on to weaken in buying power. So, for investors desiring current income from their bond investments, the stakes can be quite high.

By limiting your investments to U.S.-based bond funds, you are confined to dealing with the prevailing economic conditions in the U.S. By being open to international opportunities you allow yourself the possibility to move into different countries whose present economy may be more favorable for the type of investment you want. For example, roughly half of all bonds are located in foreign countries. If you are seeking stable income with little fluctuation, you will want to find global bond funds that are made up of bonds with short-term maturities (two years or less). Because they are short-term, they are more appropriate in meeting this need. For investors seeking solid capital appreciation with no desire for income, these funds are not as conducive to that purpose. To invest for income and growth, the most appropriate types of international bond funds are those with intermediate or long-term portfolio maturities. Considering the usual risks associated with foreign investment, I would suggest the use of intermediate-term bond funds. These vehicles contain bonds whose mid-level maturities (6–8 years) offer the best blend of volatility and capital appreciation potential.

In addition to interest risk, the international bond investor must consider the effects of market risk and credit risk. Credit risk is a risk type unique to bond funds. For international investments, you would do well to consider funds consisting of government-backed bonds from credit-worthy nations. Global bond funds that invest extensively in corporate debt securities must be examined carefully. Regulatory problems with foreign companies may prevent you from gaining an accurate reading of the credit-worthiness of the companies. High-yield bond funds (corporate "junk") are more appropriate when they are made up of domestic bonds.

International stock mutual funds, like their U.S. counterpart, are easily the most popular and widely-known of all mutual funds. These are the funds that enable you to make (and lose) the most money, and which offer you the most choices in order to satisfy your individual investment goals. They are the most interesting and the most exciting, and the foreign versions offer opportunities for building wealth. International equity funds are also the ones that require the most diligent research, by both fund manager and prospective investor. Risk factors may be quite numerous and fund objectives vary widely.

Dollars & Sense: International stock mutual funds come in three basic types:

1. Those which are diversified over a wide area (United States and a minimum of three major foreign markets);

2. Those which diversify over a particular region (European, Pacific Rim); and

3. Those which allow the investor to target one specific foreign market. The last type is more commonly known as a *single-country fund* (Mexico fund, Korea fund).

What, specifically, should you consider when analyzing international stock funds? We've already discussed the most significant risk factors that are applicable to foreign funds. The chief consideration should be the economic conditions and, specifically, market conditions of the various nations. For example, if you are looking for more aggressive growth, you know that you will be better off by considering funds that represent smaller, growth-oriented markets. A fund that includes U.S. companies and also diversifies across Germany, Japan, and Great Britain would not likely match those goals. In this case you would be better off looking at a fund that targets a relatively untapped region or country, such as Chile.

Staying abreast of international political and economic current events becomes very important to the international investor, and you would do well to read some of the better investment trade papers and periodicals. For example, *Barron's*, which is published weekly, offers a thorough run-down of activity in foreign markets, and regularly features interviews with foreign investment specialists offering their opinions of what lies ahead. Once you have targeted a specific area, you must obtain prospectuses of the funds that you have considered to be most representative of your goals. Read the prospectus carefully. Do not write off the prospectuses as a bunch of "legalese." They really are not that difficult to comprehend, and you need to know what you are buying. Pay close attention to the section on "investment objectives." Should you have any questions, do not hesitate to call the mutual fund for clarification.

While I believe that using a market "timing" method is essential for maximizing returns, I know that some of you will still opt for the more traditional "buy and hold" approach. If you are inclined to pick an investment and more-or-less "forget" about it, I would suggest you at least take the time to examine a few factors. International funds used in this manner must be broad-based, incorporating several markets into the portfolio. Long-term track records are important even though many international funds are new. If possible, find performance results for a fund over 1-, 3-, 5-, and 10-year time periods. I prefer funds with long-term successful track records paying closer attention to the fund that has an excellent 10-year performance and is also still performing well today. No matter what its past performance has been, if it's not doing well today, it's not worthwhile. Things change quickly overseas and I don't think it's a place to go bottom fishing for weak performers and wait for a bounce back. You might have a long wait.

Instead of a buy and hold strategy I would recommend international fund investors follow the market strategy discussed in the Profitline Strategy chapter. This strategy works equally well for domestic and international funds and provides a way to not only monitor the performance of your investment, but also to protect your downside risk.

CLOSED-END COUNTRY FUNDS

Closed-end country funds warrant their own separate discussion because their structure is a bit different from that of more traditional open-end funds. The best way to understand closed-end funds is to remember that mutual funds are investment companies. When you own shares of a mutual fund, you are not a shareholder in the many companies whose stocks make up the given mutual fund portfolio. Instead, you are a shareholder in the investment company (mutual fund) and you may share in the profits of the company (profits that come from investment in the securities of other companies).

Remembering that mutual funds are companies helps you to see how shares of closed-end funds are transacted. Closed-end funds offer a fixed number of shares that are publicly traded on the major exchanges. That is why they are "closed-end." Like any other company, a closed-end fund has a regulated system of capital makeup, and its shares are first dispensed through an IPO (initial public offering). The company (fund) takes the money from the initial sale of shares and invests it in individual securities in accordance with its stated goals. Open-end funds are different because their shares are offered continuously and redeemed on demand from the public. If there are many quality no-load and low-load fund families offering international investment opportunities, why would we even consider the more complicated and expensive process of closed-end fund investing? Because some of the most exciting and potentially profitable foreign opportunities may be found through such single-country closed-end funds. Many of the emerging markets that are closed to direct securities investment by foreigner's can be accessed through the funds of these markets. The Korea fund, which is traded on the New York Stock Exchange, is an excellent example of this. The Mexico fund and emerging Mexico funds are two ways to take advantage of the current growth in that market, doing so while taking advantage of some semblance of diversification. There are also single-country funds that are not closed-end (Japan by itself is represented by several traditional fund families), and these should also be considered.

Single-country closed-end funds also have an additional element of risk not encountered with open-end funds. It is the risk associated with the trading of the shares at a discount or premium. Interestingly, closed-end funds rarely trade at their net asset value (NAV). Their price is determined by the demand for their shares. Usually, the computed NAV is above the actual share price of the fund. In that case, the fund is said to be trading at discount. That characterization, however, must be taken with a grain of salt. An investor who feels he's getting a good deal by purchasing shares at a discount should remember that the shares may continue to trade below their NAV for several years. The benefit of buying at a "cheaper price," understanding that no direct connection exists between NAV and actual share price, may never be realized. Remember, too, that closed-end funds must be accessed through a broker, and I would suggest always using a discount broker.

PULLING IT ALL TOGETHER

Up to this point we have discussed some of the more specific, mechanical aspects to foreign fund investment. Now it is time to examine how these funds should be incorporated into a securities portfolio that is properly diversified.

Most financial planners feel that international funds should make up no more than 30% of any mutual fund portfolio. That's probably a reasonable figure, given the risks we discussed earlier in this study. The less diversified foreign portfolios will carry the greater risk. Single-country funds representing growth-oriented markets like the Chile fund and Mexico fund are examples. These funds should make up the smallest percentage of a portfolio because of their volatility. I would suggest regarding them as you would sector funds (health care, technology, leisure, etc.), allocating no more than 15% of your overall securities portfolio to them.

More diversified international funds can receive a larger percentage of your mu tual fund allocation. Depending on whether or not you use single-country funds, you can potentially allocate 15%–40% of your mutual fund portfolio to better diversified funds. Pay attention to the fund's objectives, and the areas of the world from which the fund may purchase securities.

WHERE TO TURN FOR INVESTMENTS

The following are some fund families and foreign fund options you may want to consider. The fund families that I will identify and describe are all suitable for satisfying your mutual fund goals. However, the individual funds named are not to be construed as blanket recommendations. Rather, they should be regarded as examples of funds from recommended families. As you invest in international funds you will also likely find that you need to branch out past some of the major fund families that you are used to. There is certainly nothing wrong with doing that. Just be careful to look at the history of the fund, its performance, and the managers experience.

Fidelity Investments
82 Devonshire Street
Boston, MA 02109
1-800-544-6666

The Fidelity mutual funds offer the greatest selection of any mutual fund family anywhere. While a few of their funds can still be purchased on a no-load basis, they most commonly possess front-end loads of 2%–3%. For a complete list of Fidelity International Funds, see Table 14-1.

Invesco Funds
P.O. Box 2040
Denver, CO 80201
1-800-525-8085

The Invesco mutual fund family has gained tremendous popularity over the past few years. Why? Because this family of funds, while maintaining a policy of "no-load" for all funds, offers considerable flexibility with respect to satisfying individual investment objectives. The Invesco family has one of the highest number of specialty, or sector, funds from which to choose, second only to Fidelity. These outstanding specialized funds are complemented by other more diversified funds of varying aggressiveness levels, making this family suitable for anyone. These funds are made even more accessible by the family's commitment to maintaining low minimum investment requirements. (See Table 14-1 for Invesco International Funds.)

Twentieth Century Investors
P.O. Box 419200
Kansas City, MO 64141
1-800-345-2021

Twentieth Century mutual funds are also true no-load funds with the unique characteristic of having very low minimums for fund investment. While this makes Twentieth Century a fine family for beginning investors, it is a high-quality fund family for anyone. Their selection is not high in number, but their funds are well-diversified and group-managed, ensuring consistency of management objectives. Twentieth Century has only one international fund, and it is a relatively recent entry into the market. However, due to the aspect of their group management philosophy, I am not hesitant about recommending it for consideration in your portfolio. (See also Table 14-1.)

T. Rowe Price
100 E. Pratt Street
Baltimore, MD 21202
1-800-638-5660

T. Rowe Price funds are solid, no-load investments with a fine variety of options available to satisfy many different investment objectives. (See also Table 14-1.)

Dreyfus
666 Old Country Road
Garden City, NY 11530
1-800-645-6561

The long-standing excellence and variety of the Dreyfus family makes it a very suitable selection for anyone seeking a reliable family. Several of the Dreyfus funds are guided by their own in-house investment committees. The Dreyfus funds have a wide mixture of no-load and low-load funds. The Worldwide Dollar Money Market Fund, considered by many to be the finest of its kind, issues its foreign money market instruments in U.S. currency, thereby preventing the problems associated with currency fluctuations. (See also Figure 14-1.)

Table 14-1   International Funds

FIDELITY INTERNATIONAL	**INVESCO**
Fidelity Advisor Emerg Mkts Incme—NL	INVESCO European
Fidelity Advisor Global Resources—NL	INVESCO European Small Company
Fidelity Advisor Overseas—NL	INVESCO International Growth
Fidelity Canada—3%	INVESCO Latin America
Fidelity Diversified International—3%	INVESCO Pacific Basin
Fidelity Emerging Markets—3%	INVESCO Worldwide Capital Goods
Fidelity Europe—3%	INVESCO Worldwide Communications
Fidelity Europe Cap Appreciation—3%	
Fidelity Global Balanced—NL	**T. ROWE PRICE**
Fidelity Global Bond—NL	Rowe Price European Stock
Fidelity Int'l Growth & Income—NL	Rowe Price Global Government Bond
Fidelity Japan—3%	Rowe Price International Bond
Fidelity Latin America—3%	Rowe Price International Discovery
Fidelity New Markets, Inc. —NL	Rowe Price International Stock
Fidelity Overseas—NL	Rowe Price Japan
Fidelity Pacific Basin—3%	Rowe Price New Asia
Fidelity Short-Term World Inc—NL	Rowe Price Short-Term Global, Inc.
Fidelity Southeast Asia—3%	
Fidelity Worldwide—3%	**DREYFUS**
	Dreyfus International Equity
20TH CENTURY	Dreyfus World Wide Dollar Money Fund
20th Century International Equity	

Again, these suggestions are by no means the only ones you should ever consider for international investment. The more astute you become, the more you may want to search, looking for that little-known opportunity. Remember, too, that international funds do not represent complete portfolios, and your overall mutual fund objectives must be considered when selecting a fund family.

Let's Remember This:

- ▶ Tomorrow's economy will be more global in nature and to take advantage you should understand the international markets.

- ▶ International investing gives you an alternative when the U.S. market is performing poorly.

- ▶ International investing is another element of portfolio diversification that you should consider.

MUTUAL FUND RETIREMENT ACCOUNT STRATEGIES

WHAT WE ARE GOING TO TALK ABOUT IN THIS CHAPTER:

▶ Which Retirement Plan Option Works for You

▶ How Annuities Can be Used as a Retirement Plan

▶ Why Mutual Funds Are Good Investments for Retirement Plans

The retirement plan for all Americans is in the midst of great turmoil. As a nation we have evolved from lifetime employment with the same company to a transient workforce. The gold watch and a pension is rapidly becoming a thing of the past, if not already lost. Today's employee can no longer rely on the company to help him in retirement. Indeed, not only is the existence of a pension in question, but also the stability of a job.

Not only are corporate retirement plans questionable, but social security is also in jeopardy in its current form. Although originally designed only as a supplement to an individual's retirement, social security has become the sole support for millions of Americans. Additionally, the system itself is clearly questionable as the increase in age of our population forces fewer and fewer working individuals to support a bulging number of retired workers.

The result of these two fundamental shifts in retirement funds will undoubtedly mean a change in your retirement plans. How you live out your later years will be determined by your own planning and savings. For a country of individuals never known for their savings ability, this harsh reality may come as a shock to those who don't heed the early warnings. In addition, because retirement savings are historically built through periodic savings of a portion of one's income, it takes years of savings and accumulation to build a comfortable nest egg. The inevitable conclusion to these facts is that you must take an active role in planning your retirement or you will be short when you get there.

Retirement Plans and Mutual Funds

If you have faced the reality that your planning will determine your retirement, you have two major decisions to make. The first is to decide what retirement program you will utilize in your retirement plan. The second decision will be to determine what investment will be used to fund your plan. Because this is a book on mutual funds you can imagine that they will be recommended for at least a portion of your funding investment. This will be true not only for the many reasons we have already discussed concerning why they are excellent vehicles, but also because funds are easy to use in a retirement program. This is true not only because the investment itself has a great deal of flexibility, but also because the industry has designed retirement plans and systems that easily enable investors to set up and run their own retirement plan. For example, it wasn't too many years ago that most IRAs were opened at banks. Now the mutual fund industry has made it easy and cheap to open an IRA at any mutual fund, frequently without an annual fee. The mutual fund industry has recognized that they have the right product at the right time to meet the needs of private retirement plans and they are on a campaign to capture as much of those billions of dollars that are looking to find an investment home as possible.

Dollars & Sense: Trading can be done in a retirement plan without regard to tax considerations because all taxes on earnings within a plan are deferred until money is taken out of the plan.

Retirement Plan Options

There are basically six options that you have for a retirement program:

1. IRA

2. SEP/IRA

3. Keough

4. 401-K

5. 403-B

6. Annuity

Each of the retirement options have their own requirements, advantages, and disadvantages. It isn't likely that you will be involved in all of the programs, but it is probable that you will be involved in more than one. Because of their different rules, you should try to be involved in several, taking maximum advantage of each of them.

The Individual Retirement Account Program (IRA)

The IRA is the best known of all the retirement programs. Every worker is entitled to set up an IRA (see Table 15-1 for the requirements). Most people will utilize the maximum allowable of $2,000 per year. Whether you are eligible for a full tax deduction, a partial deduction, or even no deduction on your contribution, you should fund your IRA every year. This is because all of the income you earn on that money will grow tax free until you begin withdrawing money out of your IRA. When you do, you will then pay ordinary income tax on the amount of contribution that was deductible plus tax on any earnings. Presumably this won't occur until retirement when your tax bracket is potentially lower. Consequently, over the years of accumulation, you will earn additional income on the portion of money you would otherwise have paid out in taxes. In turn, this money will also compound earnings on top of itself.

Mutual fund companies love IRA money, and other retirement money as well. The reason is simple. People rarely move their IRAs once they are set up. This means chances are that the mutual fund company will have you as a client for a long time. They won't have to send money marketing to replace your account and they know that if you are happy with your return, more than likely you will invest additional money with them. Because the added value of an IRA account is so high, most mutual funds offer them free of charge or at a very low cost. If the fund normally has a minimum dollar amount for opening an account, it is usually waived for IRAs.

How do you open an IRA with a mutual fund? Simple. Find the fund you like using the strategies covered in this book. Call the fund's toll-free number and ask for their IRA kit. They will send you a packet of information for free. If you already have an IRA account elsewhere, you can still open an account at a mutual fund because there is no limitation on the number of IRA accounts you can have. From a practical stand-point, you will likely want to consolidate accounts into the best performing. This would be particularly true if you were paying any fees on the least performing of the account. Use this time to review your current IRA account. Is it performing the way you would like? Are you paying fees on your current IRA account? How much are these fees in comparison to your return?

Dollars & $ense: Even if you no longer qualify for a deductible IRA, you should continue to make your contributions because all income grows tax-deferred.

The Simplified Employee Pension (SEP)

The SEP is like a super IRA because it allows you to invest so much more money than a regular IRA. Unfortunately, not everyone can qualify for a SEP/IRA. In order to qualify, you must be self-employed, or work for a company with 25 or fewer employ-ees and at least 50% of the employees must agree to enroll in the SEP. The purpose of this program was an attempt to equalize for self-employed individuals the retirement advantage that large corporate plans offered their employees. Under the SEP, the an-nual contribution is the lesser of $22,500 or 15% of compensation (or 13.04% of self-employment income). In addition, the individual can also make their regular IRA contributions. This generous contribution allows you to set aside more money for retirement as your income increases and offers the opportunity to build a substantial retirement nest egg. For example, a 35-year-old who started an SEP/IRA setting aside the maximum of $22,500 every year for 30 years would be able to accumulate $3,701,116 if he earned 10% per year. Add that amount to the social security and you can see a tremendous difference in how retirement is spent.

Like the IRA accounts, most mutual funds offer SEP/IRAs with very little cost for setup administration. The funds are after the long-term benefit of having your money and they are willing to forego the upfront income to get it.

THE KEOUGH PLAN

The Keough plan may be more well known than the SEP/IRA as the plan for self-employed individuals. The major difference is that Keoughs must include all employees. That means that if you are self-employed but also have employees, you must provide the same plan for your employees that you do for yourself. This can get extremely expensive and for that reason, Keoughs have not proliferated the way it was originally hoped.

Additionally, the Keough plan is considerably more complicated to set up and administer. However, this has been greatly reduced by the mutual fund companies who have had master Keough plans approved by the IRS. The funds offer these prototype plans at a huge savings in order to also capture the Keough plan for the long term. Some funds do charge for Keough plan services but at typically a fraction of what it would cost you to set up your own plan with an individual trustee. Consequently, if you qualify for a Keough (see Table 15-1) and decide to take advantage of its benefits, it is likely that you will use a mutual fund company to administer the program because of the cost savings.

401-K AND 403-B PLANS

The current mainstay for corporate retirement in America is the 401-K and 403-B. The 401-K is offered to employees of "for profit" corporations and the 403-B is offered for employees of "non-profit" corporations including hospitals, schools, and churches.

Under most of these plans, the employee is given an option of investment alternatives. These options may be as simple as one stock fund, one bond fund, one money market, plus the corporation's own stock, to a more sophisticated array of alternatives. In the past, little has been done to help educate the worker about how to allocate the money in your plan. The lack of help has resulted in both frustration and lost assets. In recent years, the laws governing pension plans have required not only greater investment options, but education for the participant, as well.

At a minimum, you should understand whether to have your money in stocks, bonds, or money markets and the knowledge you get from this book should allow you to easily make that decision. You should inquire with your company's plan manager about the rules for moving between the options and get all of the information available on the funds being offered.

Dollars & Sense: If your company offers a matching contribution plan where they contribute a certain dollar amount equal to your own savings, make sure you maximize this plan before you do any other investing. Matching dollar plans give you a built-in return that you can't get anywhere else.

If you are participating in a 401-K or 403-B plan, you should also be aware of exactly how your plan is being funded. There has been a growing concern about corporations not properly funding their plans and even borrowing money for corporate use. Obviously, this has led to major problems in corporations that fall into financial difficulties because you would only become an unsecured creditor of the company if, for some reason, the company was unable to pay back the money it borrowed from the corporate pension plan. As an unsecured creditor, you would have little chance of recovery and your retirement would have been squandered away. This is a serious problem that requires national attention. However, until legislative safeguards are forthcoming you need to be aware of where your company retirement plan is invested and make sure your account is funded. As an additional safeguard, when you change jobs or retire, you may want to take your retirement money with you in order to assure the money is safe. This can be done without penalty by rolling over your retirement plan into your own IRA outside the corporation. If you don't have a separate IRA then you can set one up specifically for this purpose, and I would encourage you to do so.

Dollars & Sense: Take an active role in your 401-K or 403-B plan. Encourage your plan administrator to establish flexible alternatives to give you the best investment solutions.

Annuities

Annuities are a form of private retirement plans. Money that you place in an annuity is not deductible, but money earned in the annuity is not taxed until you take the distribution. This tax-free compounding makes annuities a preferred investment for people who are in a higher tax bracket and looking to save for the long term. They are an excellent supplement to all other retirement plans. (See Chapter 17 for additional information.)

Table 15-1

Type of Plan	Last Date For Contribution	Maximum Contribution		When to Begin Distributions[1]
IRA	Due date of IRA owner's income tax return (NOT including extensions).	Smaller of $2,000 or taxable compensation.		April 1 of year after year IRA owner reaches age 70½.
SEP-IRA	Due date of employer's return (Plus extensions).	Smaller of $30,000 or 15%[2] of participant's taxable compensation.[3]		April 1 of year after year participant reaches age 70½.
KEOUGH	Due date of employer's return (Plus extensions).[4]	DEFINED CONTRIBUTION PLANS		Generally, April 1 of year after year participant reaches age 70½.[6]
		Employee	Self-Employed Individual	
		Money purchase: Smaller of $30,000 or 25% of employee's taxable compensation.	Money Purchase: Smaller of $30,000 or 20% of self-employed taxable compensation.	
		Profit-Sharing: Smaller of $30,000 or 15% of employee's taxable compensation.	Profit-Sharing: Smaller of $30,000 or 13.0435% of self-employed participant's taxable compensation.[5]	
		Defined Benefit Plan		
		Amount needed to provide an annual retirement benefit no larger than the smaller of $120,000 or 100% of the participant's average taxable compensation for his or her highest 3 consecutive years.		

[1] Distributions of at least the required minimum amount must be made each year if the entire balance is not distributed.

[2] 13.0435% of the self-employed participant's taxable compensation before adjustment for this contribution.

[3] Contributions are made to each participant's IRA (SEP/IRA) including that of any self-employed participant.

[4] The employer must set up the plan by the end of the employer's tax year.

[5] Compensation is before adjustment for this contribution.

[6] If the participant reaches age 70½ before 1988, distributions must begin by the year he or she retires.

LET'S REMEMBER THIS:

► Retirement plans can be used by active traders to avoid paying taxes until retirement.

► Funding your own retirement plan is essential for a comfortable retirement in the future.

► IRA's should always be funded even if you have another retirement plan and your IRA contributions are no longer deductible.

CHAPTER 16

MUTUAL FUND TAX STRATEGIES

WHAT WE ARE GOING TO TALK ABOUT IN THIS CHAPTER:

- ▶ How to Save Taxes on Your Mutual Fund Investments
- ▶ The Best Method to Use When Calculating Gain
- ▶ How to Use Losses to Save Your Taxes

Making money can be taxing. This is true not only as you pay tax to the government, but also taxing because the tax information can wear you out. I once had an investor who cancelled his managed fund portfolio with me even though we had consistently earned him a 16% annualized rate of return. As I do all of my clients, I called him up to discuss why he was canceling his account when his performance had been so good. "I just can't stand trying to figure out what my taxes are on these things (mutual funds)," he said to me. He said he'd rather go back to earning less money and have a simpler life. I knew how he felt. Not only did I know, I figured that many of my other clients felt the same so I now figure taxes for every client. The good news for you is that your taxes can be simplified—if not reduced!

**Dollars &
Sense:** Mutual funds are taxed on three different sources of income: dividends, the fund's capital gain distribution to you, and your capital gains generated on profitable sales of the funds you own.

Your Mutual Fund 1099

At the end of each year, your mutual fund will send you a 1099 on your income. This will tell you the dividends earned and the fund's short- and long-term capital gains. Short-term capital gains are for profits on funds held less than one year. They are taxed at your ordinary income rate. Long-term capital gains are taxed at a maximum of 28%.

In addition to the fund's gains, you may also have profits or losses on trades you made during the year. Your mutual fund will send you a 1099B that will tell you how much you received on the sale of shares during the course of the year. If you sold the shares before one year was up, you will be responsible for short- term capital gains. If you held the shares at least a year before selling, you will be eligible for long-term capital gain treatment, which saves you some money. Obviously, the government has attempted to create an incentive for you to invest long term.

The problem for poor recordkeepers is to figure out how much was paid for the fund in the first place. If you are lucky, you saved your statements. If you are more lucky, your brokerage firm or money manager does it for you. But, if no one does, don't fret, here's how to do it. There are essentially three ways to figure your gain on any sale:

1. First-In-First-Out (FIFO). This method of calculation is pretty straight-forward if you save your statements. You simply assume that the first shares you sold were the first ones you bought. For example, you buy 250 shares of Clean Air, Inc. at $20 per share, and later another 100 shares at $25 per share. If you then sold 100 shares at $30, you would assume that those 100 shares were part of the first 250 you bought and your basis would be $20. Therefore, your gain would be $10 ($30-$20=$10) and it would be a long-term gain if you had held the shares for a year and a short-term gain if you held them less than a year.

2. Specifying Shares. Using this method, you actually designate specific shares to be sold. This method allows you to pick the shares you want to sell based

on the tax ramifications best for your account. Unfortunately, it requires you to be a great recordkeeper and to give specific instructions when you sell.

3. **Average Price Per Share.** The third option is the most common because it is the easiest to calculate. You simply take the total cost of all the shares you have purchased, divide it by the number of shares and you have your average cost. Deduct the cost from the sale price and you have your gain. Once you elect to use an average basis, you must continue to use it for all accounts in the same fund. However, you may use a different method for shares in other funds, even those within the same family of funds. (See Figure 16-1.)

Figure 16-1 How to Figure Basis of Shares Sold

This is an example showing two different ways to figure basis.
It compares the FIFO method and the average basis (single-category) method.

Date	Action	Share Price	# of Shares	Shares Owned
02/04/94	Invest $4,000	$25.00	160	160
08/05/94	Invest $4,800	$20.00	240	400
12/16/94	Reinvest $300 dividend	$30.00	10	410
09/29/95	Sell $6,720	$32.00	210	200
FIFO	1. **FIFO**: To figure the basis of the 210 shares sold on 09/29/95, use the share price of the first 210 shares you bought, namely the 160 shares you purchased on 02/04/94 and 50 of those purchased on 08/05/94. $4,000 (cost of 160 shares on 02/04/94) +1,000 (cost of 50 shares on 08/05/94) $5,000 = **Basis**			
AVERAGE BASIS	2. **AVERAGE BASIS** (single-category): To figure the basis of the 210 shares sold on 09/29/95, use the average basis of all 410 shares owned on 09/29/95. $9,100 (cost of 410 shares) ÷ 410 (number of shares) $22.20 (average basis per share) $22.20 x 210 $4,662 = **Basis**			

Phantom Profits

Throughout this book, I talk about various timing scenarios for buying a particular fund. One important time period is just before the declared ex-dividend date of a fund. This is normally near the end of the year and it is always advisable to check with a fund if you are buying near that time.

The reason for the concern is that the ex-dividend date is the day used to deduct distributions from the price of your fund. The owner of the shares for the entire year is the owner on the ex-dividend date. If you buy shares just prior to that date, you will be awarded the tax distributions for the year and your shares will be adjusted. While the adjustment neutralizes any actual gain or loss, you will have to report and pay taxes on your pro-rata portion of the fund's reported gains even though you didn't hold the fund for the entire year. If this sounds confusing, that's because it is. Unfortunately, the only way to avoid this accounting profit is to avoid purchasing just before the ex-dividend date.

Losses and Deductions

Although no loss is a good loss, you don't want to just forget them. Any loss you can't use to offset gains this year should be carried forward to future years and used to offset future gains.

In addition to your investment losses, you can also deduct investment-related expenses from your income. These expenses include:

- ► Fees for investment advice and management.

- ► Subscriptions for books, newsletters, and magazines relative to your investment.

- ► Computer equipment if used to manage your investments.

- ► IRA and retirement account custodial fees.

- ► Fees related to a professional who assists you with your investment planning including attorneys, CPAs, investment advisors, etc.

- ► Seminars relating to investments including your travel and entertainment expenses (subject to the 80% deduction limit).

The above deductions do, however, carry a limitation. All the deductions must be added up and the deductible is the amount that exceeds 2% of your adjusted gross income. Because this threshold is so high, you may want to try and lump the payments for several years into one by prepaying certain items or delay paying some to get them into another year where you have a lot of expenses.

INVESTMENT INTEREST EXPENSE

In addition to the investment expenses previously mentioned, you can also deduct interest on money to buy or carry investments. While this would naturally include interest on a margin account (an account where money is borrowed from the broker), it would also include interest paid to another source where you borrowed money to invest, such as your bank. Because interest for investment purposes is deductible, and interest on consumer and personal borrowings is not, it makes sense to make sure your borrowing relates to your investments and not your consumer purchases.

The amount of money you can deduct as investment interest may be limited by two factors. One, you cannot deduct interest on money that you borrow to buy or carry shares in a mutual fund that distributes only tax-exempt interest dividends. If the fund distributes both taxable and tax-exempt dividends you must allocate the interest between the two.

The second way interest deductions are limited is by the amount of investment income. Your deduction for investment interest expenses is limited to the amount of your net investment income only. However, any unused deduction can be carried over to future years. For a complete explanation and examples, order Publication 564 "Mutual Fund Distributions." This free publication is available from the Internal Revenue Service by calling 1-800-TAX-FORM.

WASH SALE LOSSES NOT DEDUCTIBLE

One type of loss that is not deductible is one generated by selling shares and then buying back the same fund within thirty days. If you do this and the sale results in a loss, you will not be able to deduct the loss because it is washed out by the purchase. This rule is called the "Wash Sale Rule." The Wash Sale Rule does not keep you from buying another fund, including one that had a similar makeup as the one you sold. You just can't buy the same fund.

One area of the rule where many people get confused is when they sell a portion of their shares in a fund and they are also using an automatic dividend retirement plan. If the plan buys you more shares during the 30-day period you will have accidentally lost your deduction. One way around the problem is to temporarily cancel your dividend reinvestment and have the fund pay your dividends in cash.

Trading Account Gains

Frequently, investors have a trading account and a separate account for long-term holdings. Normally, the retirement account is viewed as the more conservative and the personal account more active. The problem with this approach is that it works exactly opposite of the best strategy, from a tax viewpoint.

If active trading is conducted in your personal account, you will pay consistent short capital gains tax. If instead, you conduct your active trading in your qualified retirement account, all the gains will be postponed. The reason is that you aren't taxed on gains in your qualified retirement account until you withdraw the money, and then the money is taxed as ordinary income.

While using your retirement account for active trading does offer the best tax strategy, I have sometimes been criticized for suggesting it because it puts your retirement account at a greater risk than passive accounts, and losses in the account can't be used to save on current taxes. My response is that the additional risk is minimized when compared to the potential rewards and you should never do anything simply because it might generate a loss.

Dollars & Sense: Depending on your marginal tax bracket, an investor may do better from an after-tax return to buy tax-free municipals instead of taxable bonds. Always make your final analysis based on "after-tax yields" instead of "pre-tax" yields.

Individual Retirement Account Distributions

Sooner or later you have to pay the piper for all the taxes you deferred in your IRA or other qualified retirement plan. You may begin withdrawing money out of your plan without penalty at age $59^1/_2$ and you must start withdrawals no later than age $70^1/_2$ or you also start paying a penalty.

Like most tax situations, you will have choices of how you receive the income from your IRA. You can either receive income based on your life expectancy or you can use the joint life expectancy of you and your beneficiary. If you want to take out as little money as possible for now, use the joint life expectancy if your beneficiary is younger because the blended age will be lower.

Your second decision is whether you want to use a term-certain (fixed number of years) or if you want to recalculate the term length for distribution. If you use term-certain, you simply look at the age table the first year, divide the number of remaining years you have into your money available, and you will get your distribution. The next year you use one year less to divide by.

If you elect to recalculate every year, you get a slight advantage on the mortality tables because an actuary who knows these things has decided that your life expectancy doesn't really decrease by a full year every 12 months. (Don't ask me to explain why.) However, when both the holder and the beneficiary die, the next person in line must take all remaining dollars and immediately pay taxes on it with no deferral. Thus, for most people, the term-certain is the preferred method.

LET'S REMEMBER THIS:

▶ Always try to defer your taxes, which will increase your after-tax yield.

▶ Never make an investment decision just because it will save taxes.

▶ Restructure your loans from consumer interest that is non-deductible to investment interest that is deductible.

How to Defer Taxes on Your Mutual Funds Using Annuities

What We Are Going to Talk About in This Chapter:

- ▶ The Advantages and Disadvantages of Annuities
- ▶ The Difference Between Fixed Annuities and Variable Annuities
- ▶ How to Use Annuities to Create Your Own Private Retirement Account

If I were going to design a perfect investment, I would sit down and make a list.

First I would want some safety. I realize that there is a give-and-take between risk and reward, but because I am doing the designing, that is what I would want on my list.

Next, I would like liquidity. Sometimes you need cash and access is important. This would be less important if I had other money that I could access but, in general, it would be on my list to some degree.

A tax shelter would also be on the list. I know money that grows tax-deferred winds up with a bigger pot than money that I have to pay taxes on.

A guarantee is also important. While this wish is similar to safety, it gives me a better feeling to know that someone is backing up their investment.

Flexibility would be important, too. I know that there is no investment that is the best for all times so I want to be able to move between investments whenever necessary.

I would like the investment to be no-load (meaning no commission or up-front fee). I don't mind paying people for their service, but I would rather not pay a big chunk out of my money upfront before anything happens. I hate it when someone makes more on my money than I do.

Creditor protection would also be on my list. In this lawsuit-happy world it would be nice to design an investment that would protect me from unforeseen accidents or business problems that might spill over to my personal life.

Finally, I'd like to be able to use this investment as an estate planning vehicle and totally avoid probate, thus saving up to 10% in additional costs and expenses.

Sounds great, doesn't it? Too bad, you say, there is not one of these ideal investments. Well, I am happy to say that there is. Interestingly, it comes to us from an unlikely source. Insurance companies.

Yes, the insurance industry has been able to utilize their powerful lobbying organization to alter one of their old stand-by products, annuities, into today's super-annuity. While many investors are turning their noses at what they think is an old, stale, fixed annuity, they should be paying close attention to what has now happened to the annuities. Unlike any other investment, they really do have all of the benefits we just mentioned. Additionally, because of their structure, annuities offer an excellent method for you to establish your own private retirement program to supplement your qualified retirement plan and social security.

Two Types of Annuities: Fixed and Variable

The *fixed annuity* is like a tax-free CD. You lock in a pre-set return that you are willing to receive on your money and you sit back and let it grow. But different from a CD, a fixed annuity, sometimes called the annuity CD, grows tax-deferred. This means you don't pay taxes until you start spending the money. Each and every year your money builds without paying taxes. So, your money makes you money, the money you would be paying to taxes makes you money, and your interest makes you money. Sort of a triple whammy. Typically, like a CD, you can lock in interest rates. The normal time period is for one, three, and five years. Some programs offer other possibilities, but these are the normal time frames.

Fixed annuities usually have a guaranteed minimum rate which is called the floor rate annuity. The insurance company promises that you won't ever get below that amount no matter what happens to interest rates. Sometimes, they also have an interest rate bail out clause. This option is good because it allows you to get out of the annuity without any penalty, if interest rates fall below a certain pre-set amount.

One problem with the fixed annuity is the stated rate of payment. In many cases, annuities offer a stated rate of payment which, in reality, acts as a "teaser rate" for the first year. After you've been in the annuity for a year, your pay rate adjusts and as you can imagine, it is not usually upward. Before you purchase a fixed annuity, investigate what the current adjustments are for the annuities placed a year ago. This rate will give you a better idea of what you can expect your actual rate to be. You can bet it won't be as good as the stated rate they are quoting you.

Money Talks: A fixed annuity provides a guaranteed minimum by an insurance company. A variable annuity is invested in mutual funds and its return is dependent on the success of the mutual fund.

The second type of annuity is the *variable annuity*. It functions like a tax-free mutual fund. Your annuity allows you to invest your money in a variety of mutual funds and because it is under the annuity umbrella, the money grows tax free until you take it out of the annuity.

The mutual fund selection offered by the annuities are like fund families. Generally, you may choose between stock funds, bond funds, and money markets. Some plans have greater flexibility and allow international investing as well as more speculative sector fund investing. Obviously, all things being the same, the greater the flexibility in fund selection, the better the annuity.

Dollars & Sense: Use variable annuities as a way to combine mutual fund investing on a tax deferred basis.

THE EIGHT FEATURES OF A GREAT ANNUITY

Now that you have the basic type of annuities outlined, lets go back to our original wish list for an ideal investment and see how our annuities stack up.

Remember, here are the points we were looking for:

1. Safety

2. Liquidity

3. Tax Shelter

4. Guarantee

5. Flexibility

6. No-Load

7. Creditor Protection

8. Estate Planning

I'm sure you will agree that this is a great wish list. Let's go through each of these and see how they apply to the annuity.

SAFETY

Is an annuity safe?

Annuities are an insurance investment product. Consequently, you need to look at the insurance company to determine your financial backing. As to safety, it also makes a difference whether the annuity is fixed or variable.

The news media has caused some concern about insurance companies. When our nightly anchorman asks the question whether insurance companies are going the way of the S & L's, you have an example of media sensationalism at its best, or worst as the case may be. Don't get me wrong, we may have insurance company failures, but in recent years television has suggested a collapse of the entire insurance industry. If that occurs, the country will be having such serious financial problems, that any investment you might be in would be equally hurt. The only "safe" place in that case might be U.S. Government Treasuries and your money's value would be so ruined by inflation and taxes that you wouldn't have anything left in the long run.

No, I don't think we are going to have an insurance industry failure, but you do need to look at the individual insurance company from which you buy your annuity because there is no justification for ignoring any potential risk.

Dollars & Sense: Use independent rating services to help you determine the safety of any annuity you review.

Independent rating services make our life easier when it comes to picking an insurance company. There are several, including A.M. Best, Moody's, Standard & Poor's, and Duff and Phelps. These services rate the companies on their overall financial health. The company that is "A" or better from A.M. Best, or "AA" or better from Standard & Poor's, and "Aa" or better from Moody's, should give you adequate comfort. If you want even more security, request the higher ratings. In addition to the current year's rating, also look at the previous year's ratings. If a company was downgraded from its previous year's rating I would consider that a bad sign and make it a point to find out why.

If you are still concerned, you can also make a quick call to both your state insurance commissioner and the state where the insurance company is incorporated. All states maintain an insurance company watch list. This list would help you know if there are a large number of complaints against the company or if they are not following governmental reserve requirements. While the state will tell you that they also have a state insurance fund to protect you in case the company has financial trouble, these funds don't have the backing of the federal government and like many state accounts, are simply under-funded. While you might get your money back, "when" you get it back could be an important question to ask.

Most of your concern for the financial condition of the insurance company relates to an investment in a fixed annuity product. The reason for this is because the money invested in a fixed annuity is taken by the insurance company and invested by the company. If there is a problem, you must look to the assets of the insurance company for collection and in a bankruptcy, you would only be treated as a general creditor.

On the other hand, a variable annuity is a segregated investment. The insurance company must put your money in an account totally segregated or separate from the general assets of the company. Then, in case of bankruptcy by the company, general creditors would have no right of access to these funds. Consequently, if you invested in a variable annuity, your safety concern should be more with how your investment is doing and less about the financial stability of the insurance company. Nevertheless, prudence dictates that you follow the credit rating report as I previously discussed.

LIQUIDITY

If an emergency arises, can I get my money? This is a frequently asked question, especially by retirees. Depending on the total amount of money a person has available for investment, the uncertainties of life frequently dictate a need for access. Annuities provide you with this type of emergency protection.

Like many good things in life, immediate access has some strings attached. The basic rule is that until you are 59 $\frac{1}{2}$, any withdrawal will cost you a penalty of 10% of the amount withdrawn, payable to the IRS. This is the same penalty charged on your IRA or other retirement program that you may have for similar early withdrawals. Additionally, you will now have to pay income tax on money withdrawn because it wasn't taxed in the annuity. The final hit may come from the insurance company that normally has surrender charges the first few years of your investment. Typically, these are reducing charges.

ANNUITY SURRENDER CHARGES

The list below is an example of annuity surrender charges. In this case, if you surrendered the annuity in the third year, you would pay a 4% redemption fee.

6%	Year 1
5%	Year 2
4%	Year 3
3%	Year 4
2%	Year 5
1%	Year 6
Zero thereafter	

At first glance, the penalties look high. They are. Remember, however, that no one wants an annuity to be set up for a short time—neither the insurance company, nor the government, nor you for that matter. Most annuities should be viewed as long-term investments. Otherwise you are not using the advantages of tax-free compounding in the first place. Consequently, the penalties discourage you from using this money. However, if you need it you know you can get it.

There is one major exception to the IRS's 10% penalty, and it is a big one. If you are medically diagnosed with an illness of 30 days or more, or you become disabled, then you will not be penalized. This is a tough way of getting out of a 10% penalty, but it is a good safety net. Because the main reason most people are concerned about emergency access is for medical reasons, this will probably provide you with enough comfort. The real key point to remember here is that you will have liquidity if you need it.

Dollars & Sense: **PLANNING STRATEGIES** Because the 10% penalty is levied on withdrawals before the age of 59 1/2, many investors past that age also use annuities for short-term goals. New products are structured more like CDs and do not have the longer withdrawal penalties previously mentioned. These investments, frequently called CD Annuities, allow you to get yields slightly higher than CDs but are tax-deferred until you use the money.

Tax Shelter

Hesitating to be repetitive, let me say that tax deferral is a big advantage to annuities. You are earning interest on your money that you would have paid to Uncle Sam, and that interest is also earning money. This is clearly additional money that you would have not have made outside the annuity.

Eventually, when you start receiving payouts from your annuity, some of the money will be taxable income and some will be considered non-taxable return of principal. Remember that part of the check you are getting is part of the original investment that you paid into the plan and you already paid taxes on that amount. To determine how much money you must pay, the IRS has issued rules that define the exclusion ratio to determine the amount of taxes owed. Don't be concerned about the complications of all this because it will be done automatically for you. Every calculation will be different because it is based on a formula that compares your life expectancy, the amount of your original investment, and the present value of your investment account. Sometimes I wonder who stays up all night developing these formulas. It doesn't weigh heavy on my mind, and shouldn't on yours.

Dollars & $ense: Because you don't pay capital gains on annuities you need not concern yourself with the tax consequences of trading or switching between your investments held in the annuity.

GUARANTEE

We all know that there are guarantees and then there are "guarantees." The important question is who is guaranteeing what.

The best type of guarantee is the United States Government. It is also the most expensive. By expensive I mean that anytime you get a U.S. Government guarantee, the interest you earn will not keep your money up to its original amount after calculations for inflation and taxes. In fact, because of inflation and taxes, what you are guaranteed is that you have an eroding amount of principal. Many investors do not think this through. These investors are so concerned about the possibility of not getting a return on their original investment, that in reality, they settle for just that. Fear makes poor investment decisions.

There are two types of guarantees associated with an annuity:

1. A fixed rate guarantee with a return of principal.

2. A death benefit guarantee.

The *fixed rate guarantee* is provided by the insurance company for investors who want the assurance of pre-set returns. The issuing insurance company takes the risk that they can take your money and make more money on it than they are paying you. The important issue for the investor is to assure themselves that the guarantee is good. This means you must investigate the insurance company as discussed earlier in the section on safety.

The *death benefit guarantee* is an advantage exclusive to annuities. The insurance company takes a small portion of your money and, in effect, covers you with an insurance policy. With this protection, the insurance company can now say that the value of your principal will not go down past your original investment if you die before withdrawing the money. This means if you invest the money, even in a variable annuity, and the market crashes, your heirs would get no less than 100% of your original investment if you were to die before the investment recovered. I know, death is a tough way to beat the stock market, but it does provide tremendous protection for families who might otherwise be reluctant to make investments. Additionally, most policies allow for increasing protection. This means that as your portfolio increases in value after a certain number of years, the insurance company will give you this higher amount as a death benefit minimum.

Particularly for investors with discretionary money, those who are building an estate to pass on either to their children or to a charity, this benefit allows them to be a little more aggressive, seeking higher returns, but knowing that in reality the value of the money that their heirs or the charity ultimately receives will not be diminished.

FLEXIBILITY

One of the major problems with long-term investments is their lack of flexibility. In other words, once invested you are locked in to that investment. Not true with an annuity. Annuities are simply the umbrella under which you invest. The annuities offer a variety of investment options under the tax-deferred umbrella and you can frequently switch between the investment options offered. Most annuity plans now offer stock funds, bond funds, and money markets. Many are now expanding with international stock and bond alternatives along with more aggressive sector fund options. The point is, as the economy and markets change, so can your annuity investments without any penalties, fees, or taxes.

NO-LOAD

Investors are becoming more conscious of large up-front fees that are required for investments. They have come to realize that it takes a long time to recover from not having 100% of your money working for you. As a result, over the years we have seen new trends develop with discount brokerage services and no-load mutual funds. Annuities are following this tradition. Almost all annuities are sold as no-load or no up-front commission. That does not mean that there are no fees or costs associated with an annuity. There are administrative fees, management fees, and mortality and risk fees that are all charged on an annual basis and in the same manner that mutual funds deduct their fees. The insurance company uses these fees to pay the operational expenses of the fund, to pay for the death benefit we discussed, and pay for sales and marketing expenses that they have paid up front to get you involved. Typically, the total amount of these annual fees will run between 2%–3% annually. In the past couple of years, some large mutual fund companies have brought out their own line of annuities that they market as "pure no-load." This means that no money is being paid out by the sponsor to anyone for marketing. Consequently, these companies are likely to charge less annual expenses because they didn't have to pay out a marketing expense on your sale. Like all fees and expenses, shop around for the plan that offers you the best deal and don't assume that even an annuity promoted as "no load" is automatically the cheapest. You will have to compare the annual fees as well.

Annuities also frequently have surrender charges in addition to the annual fees. As discussed earlier, these fees are charged if you need to get out of the annuity early. The insurance company has likely paid a commission to someone for selling you the annuity. If you get out early, they charge the surrender fees to recover the cost of getting you as a customer.

CREDITOR PROTECTION

As you know by now, annuities are insurance products. As such, states give them additional protection against lawsuits and bankruptcies, which gives you added protection. In some states, Florida for example, any money you have invested in an annuity would be totally protected from creditors. Consequently, all professionals who have a high degree of exposure to malpractice claims should reconsider annuities as a major investment planning vehicle. Because annuities are controlled by state regulators, the specific laws that provide this protection do vary from state to state. For specifics on the protection that an annuity might offer you in a particular state, you can call your state insurance commissioner or discuss it with your personal planner.

ESTATE PLANNING

Although estate planning is not a major reason for investing in an annuity, it is a big additional benefit.

Annuities avoid probate, plain and simple. Any annuity policy that has not been annuitized (started paying out over your lifetime) will pass, upon your death, to your stated beneficiary without going through probate. There are a few states that do not offer this benefit. A simple call to your local probate court will give you the answer. (You can get the number by calling your local directory assistance.) Avoiding probate on this asset can save you as much as 15% in probate expenses, attorneys fees, and court costs on the assets. It will also save a great deal of time because probate can extend from one to ten years or even longer in complicated cases. Additionally, because the amount of asset is excluded from your estate, this would give you cash to pay any estate taxes that might be due. All estate taxes are due within nine months after death, and if probate has not been settled, your family will have to come up with the cash from other sources. This could cause extreme hardship and force sale of valuable properties. The annuity asset could prevent this problem from occurring.

Dollars &	Use annuities as an additional private retirement program. Although your initial contribution is not tax deferred, the money you make on it in the annuity grows tax deferred.
Sense:	

Advanced Annuities Strategies

1. Maximize Your Return With Variable Annuities

    I'm not going to come out and say that no one should buy a fixed annuity, but I just can't think of anyone who should.

    People who buy fixed annuities do so only because of fear. They trade larger potential returns for comfort. The only problem is that like fixed instruments, including CD's, your real adjusted return after inflation is not very good.

    Variable annuities may not be better every year. However, because this is the long-term investment program that will have the benefit of averaging the peaks and valleys of stock and bond markets, you will do better over a long period with the variable annuity. Remember, variable annuities are now managed and run by some of the best money managers in America. In the short term, anyone can make a mistake, but over the long term, these professionals have historically proven themselves.

2. How to Improve on Your Money Manager's Return

    Most variable annuities divide their investment alternatives into three basic types: stocks, bonds, and money markets. You can sometimes add sub-category alternatives to this, such as international stocks and bonds or sector (specialized stock) funds.

    As previously discussed, there is no single, good long-term investment. For example, as interest rates are falling, bonds are an excellent investment. In a falling interest rate environment your bond will make money on the interest, plus you will earn capital gain profits. The capital gain profits will come as your bond portfolio of higher yielding bonds are sold at a premium. Unfortunately, however, interest rates also rise. If you invest when the mutual fund holds lower interest rate bonds, as rates rise your portfolio becomes worthless. If you remain in the bond account for the entire time, your highs and lows will tend to average out and you will generally earn the bond interest only. How do you maximize your return? By moving out of the bond fund when interest rates start to rise, and into the bond fund when interest rates fall. If you make only that one switch (move), then you will increase your overall return dramatically with capital gain profits.

Where do you switch to? Your alternative will be to move to any of the other funds that are performing better or to your money market account as a temporary resting place. This movement between funds is called "Money Movement." It can be treated simply as we have just done, or we can add combinations and variables using advanced formulas. (See Chapter 11, "The Profitline Strategy," and Chapter 10, "How the Economy and Interest Rates Effect Your Mutual Fund Return.")

How do you make the switch? Annuities make switching simple. All that is required is to call the insurance company toll free and tell them where you want to move and into which fund you want your money moved. Many companies allow unlimited switching. Some restrict you to 10 or 12 a year. You really don't need more than 2 or 3 switches in most years.

3. Riskless Annuities

What if I could show you a way to invest in a variable annuity, but I will guarantee that you won't lose any of your principal? Would you be interested? What's the catch, right? Well, the catch is that if your variable annuity does really well, you won't make quite as good of a return as you would have if you had invested entirely in that variable annuity. You are going to give up some of that additional return for additional safety.

This safety plan is called a "split annuity." You use about one-third of your total investment and put it into a fixed account. This account will be guaranteed to grow back to your original total investment amount over a certain period. The balance of your investment will be put into a variable annuity and follow the advanced strategies that we have discussed. Now, here is the result. If your variable annuity crashed and went to virtually nothing, your fixed side would restore your original investment. (Also remember that when you die, your death benefit would also restore the variable's side for your heirs.) On the other hand, if your variable annuity does as well as we would expect, then your fixed rate side would simply add to your overall return. If this sounds like a safe way to invest, that's because it really is. This method of splitting an annuity provides everything you need in an investment.

4. The Lifetime Gift

Over the years, parents and grandparents have always given money to their children. When they could afford it, they frequently took advantage of the $10,000 per person per year gift tax exclusion. More often than not, this money is quickly spent.

The best strategy to use here is to adopt the concept used by major financial and educational institutions for years—the endowment. In this case, the private endowment.

Let's assume that grandparents decide to collectively give their newborn grandson $20,000 to start out his new life. As you will see, this will be all the money he'll ever need.

For illustration purposes, we will assume that the grandparents take the $20,000 and buy a variable annuity. The annuity will earn a 12% growth rate. At the age of 19, we will assume that the grandson withdraws $10,000 each year for four years to go to college. At age 30, he withdraws 10% of the amount in the plan to use as a down payment on a house and to get his business going. He does this for three years. At age 65 he wants a $75,000 annual income plus social security and any other benefits. Let's see how the plan helps this grandson.

Table 17-1

PV (Present Value) $20,000	I (Interest) 12%	N (Number of Years) 18 = $153,000
Year	*Distribution*	*Balance*
Age 18	(the account has grown to)	$153,000
19	($10,000 for 1st yr college)	$161,055
20	($10,000 for 2nd yr college)	$169,182
21	($10,000 for 3rd yr college)	$178,284
22	($10,000 for 4th yr college)	$188,478

For the next 8 years, no withdrawals.		(After withdrawal)
30	($41,666 for down payment)	$419,994
31	($42,000 for business)	$423,358
32	($42,354 for business)	$426,744

continues

Table 17-1 (continued)

PV (Present Value) $20,000	I (Interest) 12%	N (Number of Years) 18 = $153,000
Year	Distribution	Balance
No other withdrawals until age 65.		
65	($75,000 for income)	$17,878,325
66	($75,000 for income)	$19,939,730
67	($75,000 for income)	$22,248,490
68	($75,000 for income)	$24,834,309
69	($75,000 for income)	$27,730,426
70	($75,000 for income)	$30,974,077
71	($75,000 for income)	$34,606,967
72	($75,000 for income)	$38,675,803
73	($75,000 for income)	$43,232,899
74	($75,000 for income)	$48,336,847
75	($75,000 for income)	$54,053,269
76	($75,000 for income)	$60,466,661
77	($75,000 for income)	$67,628,340
78	($75,000 for income)	$75,667,501
79	($75,000 for income)	$84,652,401
80	($75,000 for income)	$94,726,689

While this example begins to get a little ridiculous in the total dollars of growth, it certainly illustrates the true value of tax-free compounding. Obviously, this grandson could and would increase his income above $75,000 per year. The point is, he certainly has the capability to do so. The other factor that you may have questioned is the ability of a lot of grandparents funding the original $20,000. Well, what if they only did half or even 25%? What if the parents and grandparents joined together to fund it? Obviously, the possibilities are limitless. The point is to start.

Top Rate Annuities

The following Top Rate Annuities come to us from *100 Best Investments For Your Retirement* ($6.95). A copy is available by calling 1-800-333-3700.

American Skandia Advisors Plan II 125
One Corporate Drive
Shelton, CT 06484-0883
1-800-752-6342

Investors Select
206 South 13th Street
Lincoln, NE 68508
1-800-865-5237

The Best of America IV
P.O. Box 16609
Columbus, OH 43216-6609
1-800-848-6331

Keyport Preferred Advisor
High Street
Boston, MA 02110-2712
1-800-367-3653

Commonwealth
6610 West Broad Street
Richmond, VA 23230
1-800-521-8884

Let's Remember This:

- ▶ Variable annuities offer unusual features that no other investment offers, such as creditor protection and investment guarantees.

- ▶ Trading gains are totally deferred when you use annuities.

- ▶ Annuities have unique investment strategies offered by no other investment option.

CHAPTER 18

STRATEGIES FOR THE TIMES OF YOUR LIFE

WHAT WE ARE GOING TO TALK ABOUT IN THIS CHAPTER:

► How to Apply Specific Strategies to a Variety of Circumstances

► How Portfolio Recommendations Can Vary Based on Your Goals and Objectives

► How to Conduct Your Own Financial Quick Start

The purpose of this chapter is to tie together everything I have taught you. You will analyze a case and apply what you have learned to reach a recommended strategy. You will be using the same process that we use when conducting our 30-minute Financial Quick Start for clients.

To be successful in mutual fund investing, you don't need to use all of the strategies we have discussed in this book, just the ones that work for you. You may only need one strategy because if that one helps you reach your goals, that's all you need. This chapter will quickly show you that the strategy you use will depend greatly on where you are financially in life, your age, risk tolerance, and objectives.

Throughout this book, I have tried to teach you how to handle your own mutual fund investing. Now is the time to test yourself. As you read the case study, assume you are the person seeking help. Before you read my recommendation, think about what you feel you would do if you were in this situation. Although you won't personally face every situation that is discussed, learning how to handle different situations will help you understand the strategies that were covered in this book and help cement them in your mind.

CASE STUDY NO. 1

Background:

Investor: Single male, age 25

Education: 2 years, Associate's Degree

Occupation: Real Estate Salesman

Goals: 1. Return to college and get a degree in business.

2. Save some money.

Risk Tolerance: Aggressive

Income: $28,000

Assets:		
	$1,500	IRA
	250	Cash
	500	Personal Property
	$2,250	

Liabilities:		
	$12,000	Car Loan
	4,200	Credit Card Debt
	1,000	Student Loan
	$17,200	

Net Worth: -$14,950

Recommendation:

The $4,200 in credit card debt at 19%–21% average interest on each credit card can become a major problem if your lifestyle continues to expand. The best thing you can do from an investment standpoint is take the same money you were going to set aside for mutual funds and pay off the credit cards. By paying off the credit cards, you are guaranteeing a return equal to the amount of interest you are currently paying on the cards, and no one can guarantee that amount of return in mutual funds or any other investment. The student loan is only a 9% loan and because I believe you can do better than that by investing, I would simply continue to make payments on that debt. It is a slight stretch to turn down the guaranteed return you would effectively earn paying down the 9% loan, but learning sound investing strategies has an additional value.

The best way to get started investing is to use your IRA account. You already have one set up and you should continue. Right now the IRA is in a local bank money market. You should transfer the IRA to one of the discount brokerage firms that offers no-load trading (See the Resources chapter). Next, you should arrange for a certain portion of your salary to be added to the amount each month. Try to find enough monthly income to meet your $2,000 IRA annual contribution, in addition to a monthly pay-down on your credit card. With the IRA contribution, you should start a mutual fund investment program using no-load mutual funds.

Your first investment should be based on the economic trends at the time you're ready to invest. If the market as a whole is in a down trend, you may want to invest first in a mutual fund money market or a very short-term bond fund. This move would only be temporary because as soon as possible, you need to be in growth funds. If the market is in a positive up trend, you should invest in one or two growth funds. Because of your age, you can also use aggressive growth funds. Even if they take a tumble, you have plenty of time to wait for a recovery.

Once you have earned enough money to pay off your credit card and fund your IRA, you should also consider an SEP/IRA. Because you are self-employed, the SEP will allow you to increase your annual contribution on your earnings (see Chapter 15 for more information).

Recommended Allocation for IRA:

Figure 18-1 Portfolio Recommendation

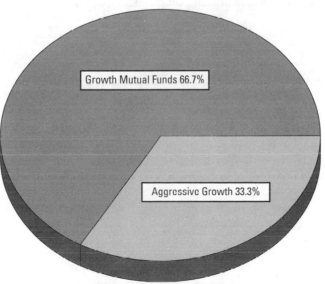

CASE STUDY NO. 2

Background:

Investor: Married couple. Husband, 32 and wife, 29. No children, but are planning to have at least two.

Education: Husband, post graduate; wife, Masters.

Occupation: Husband is a CPA, wife is a teacher

Risk tolerance: Moderate

Income: Husband: $38,000

Wife: <u>$26,000</u>

Total: $64,000

New Savings: $1,000 per month

Assets: $5,000   Equity in 2 cars

12,000   Equity in home

2,000   403-B

4,000   Personal Property

<u>1,500</u>   Cash

$24,500

Liabilities: $34,000   Car Loans

75,000   First Mortgage on Home

<u>3,000</u>   Credit Card

$112,000

Net Worth: -$87,500

Recommendation:

The profile for this young couple is not unusual today. If it fits your situation, you will need to understand that you are in a changing position. While you may not be expecting children immediately, that could change and if it does, you will need additional money. Consequently, while you can be growth oriented, you must keep a careful eye on fluctuations in market conditions. You may need your cash savings, so you don't want to create a risk that your principal may be down at the wrong time. It is very important that you understand the Profitline Strategy so you can use it to protect your down slide and preserve principal.

A good start has been made by establishing a retirement program with the school system's 403-B. As you know, it works like a 401-K program for private companies. I suggest that you continue to make contributions. You have a choice of funds that you can pick from each quarter and I recommend that you move into the growth fund account because current market conditions are good, interest rates are flat or falling, and your age and goals suggest long-term growth.

Your spouse also needs to start a retirement program and I would recommend an IRA. If you can qualify for an SEP/IRA, do that because you can increase your contribution tremendously. If you start the IRA, I recommend that you immediately fund this year's contribution instead of waiting until the end of the year. You can fund it out of the $1,000 per month savings over the next two months. Invest the IRA in a no-load growth fund that has been a consistent top performer for the past 10-, 5- and 1-year periods. You may also want to verify your selection by using one of the major mutual fund services, such as Morningstar or Value Line.

Because you are committed to saving $1,000 per month, you should immediately set up a debit program that will automatically draft money out of your savings account into the mutual fund. The money should go into the mutual funds and money market and then directed by you into the fund family's best performing fund. You should follow the Profitline Strategy as it relates to each fund in the family. During an overall down market, you may keep new money in the money market and even consider switching money you have in other funds over the money market. (On a very important note, the individual in this age bracket typically faces frequent changes in his life. Annual financial checkups are important to make sure you remain on the right track.)

Figures 18-2A–18-2C   Portfolio Recommendation

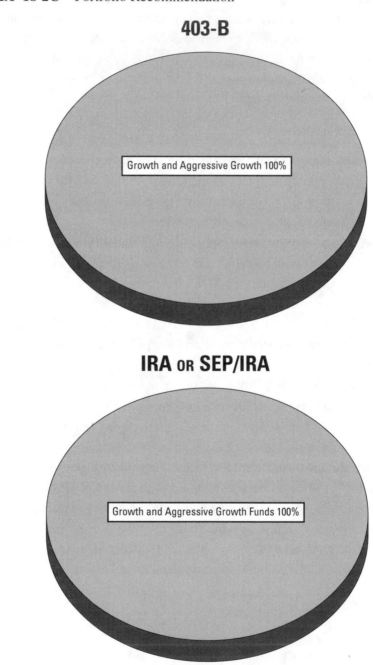

PERSONAL ACCOUNT

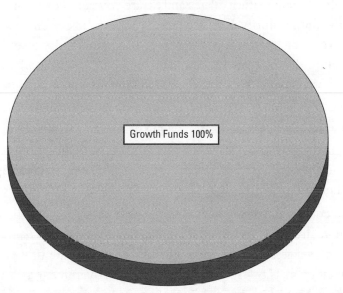

Growth Funds 100%

CASE STUDY NO. 3

Background:

Investor: Single male, age 16

Education: High School

Occupation: unemployed

Special Situation: medical disability

Goals: 1. Physical improvement from an accident.

2. Invest the money to preserve principal and have income for life in about five years.

Risk Tolerance: Conservative

Assets: $600,000 cash settlement

Liabilities: 0

Net Worth: $600,000

Recommendation:

This is a difficult case and one in which many advisors will differ. Because you place such great emphasis on safety, the easy thing to do is to recommend that the entire amount of money be placed in U.S. Treasury securities. You could layer the securities with different maturity dates and assure yourself the return by simply holding the security until maturity. Because there is no need for current income, you could even add zero coupon bonds for perhaps 5- or 10-year maturity dates and again hold until they mature. If cash was needed then you could spend it when the securities mature, or if not, reinvest. This strategy can be implemented by either buying individual treasuries or using no-load funds structured the same way.

While the treasury recommendation would be the safest method on the surface, it might not be in the long run. This is because it ignores inflation and income tax. If all of the money is invested in treasuries, the entire income may be eaten up over time by inflation and tax.

In order to counter the negative consequences of taxes and inflation, I would recommend a more diversified approach that sacrifices some short-term safety for long-term safety. My suggestion is as follows: Fifty percent of the money should be put into a combination of U.S. Treasury securities and government agency certificates. All of these are backed by the full faith and credit of the U.S. Government. Use mutual funds that have staggered maturity dates in order to minimize the effect of interest rate fluctuations in the portfolio. Twenty-five percent of the portfolio would go into mutual funds Corporate AAA bonds. These bonds are not as safe as treasuries, but you increase the yield substantially at minimal risk. A short and intermediate selection of bond funds would minimize the effect of interest fluctuations. The final 25% of the portfolio would be split into three baskets, each aimed at protecting inflation damage against your portfolio. Twelve and one-half percent would go into an S & P Index fund, six and one-quarter percent would go into a growth fund, and six and one-quarter percent would go into an international fund. The international fund might be a little more aggressive than you need, but it is an excellent counter protection to the otherwise conservative holdings. Use a very broad-based international fund or perhaps even an international index fund.

The key to this portfolio is understanding that there are different types of safety just as their are different types of risk. Most people only see the one form of safety: loss of principal due to the security's fluctuation. They forget about protecting from other dangers, like taxes, inflation, and diversification in the type of investments.

Figure 18-3 Portfolio Recommendation

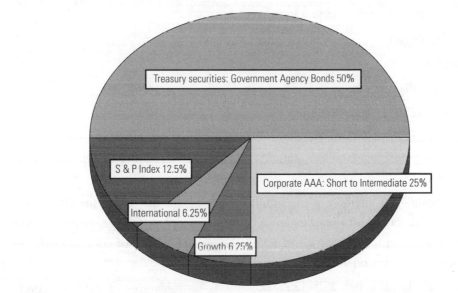

CASE STUDY NO. 4

Background:

Investors: Husband is 67 years old, wife is 65 years old, they have two children ages 36 & 39.

Education: College.

Occupation: Husband, retired and freelance business consultant.

Wife, retired.

Risk Tolerance: Moderate

Income:	$19,200	Social Security
	25,000	Consulting part-time
	12,000	Pension
	13,000	Income Investment
	$69,200	

Assets:	$175,000	IRA Rollover, Money Market, CDs
	250,000	Home, Free and Clear
	35,000	Cars, Paid For

20,000   CD, 6%

<u>15,000</u>   Money Market

Total: $495,000

Liabilities: 0

Health: Currently, excellent.

Net Worth: $495,000

From a financial standpoint, you are in very good shape. However, your investments are not producing what they should be, particularly since you have no need for current income.

At this point, your main concern should be saving for the future for either your additional needs or to build your estate. Like many people your age, you have concerns about long-term health care and acknowledge that growth of your assets is one way to provide protection.

Because the home is free and clear, should long-term health care become a problem it could be sold for cash to provide for assisted living. Consequently, because there is no need for current income, you should concentrate on growth of your liquid assets.

From a mutual fund investment strategy, I would recommend 25% growth funds, 25% S & P Index, 25% balance fund, and 25% international.

Figure 18-4   Portfolio Recommendation

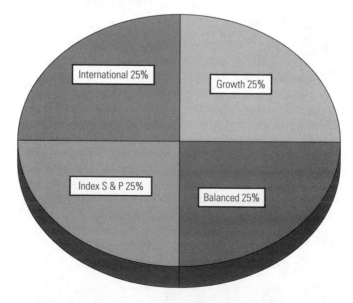

There will be some adjustments to the portfolio annually and we have discussed how to use the Profitline Strategy to make those adjustments. At the time of making the recommendation, I feel the international markets are just starting to take off and it allocates a portion of their assets to another part of the world economy. The growth fund is an inflation hedge and the index fund provides maximum diversity among the entire market. The balanced fund completes the picture by giving them some bonds without being a pure bond play. I recommend that the CDs be cashed in only when they mature to avoid the penalty for early withdrawal. I would invest the money into the market over a period of weeks to take advantage of incrementally investing, watching the direction of the market. As long as the market continues in a positive trend, I would move towards full investment.

The one thing no one asked about, but I would encourage, is some minor estate planning. You both have a will, but you need living trusts. Living trusts offer numerous advantages over a will including both privacy and probate avoidance. In this case, the living trust will allow you to totally avoid probate and increase your estate tax shelter to $1.2 million instead of $600,000. While your estate isn't high enough to even take advantage of that savings yet, successful growth over the rest of your lives could easily put it there and the trust has no disadvantage.

CASE STUDY NO. 5

Background:

Investors: Husband, 78 and wife, 77, they have 3 children ages 45, 48, & 55.

Occupation: Retired

Goals: Maintain income, preserve principal

Risk tolerance: Conservative

Health: OK

Income:	$19,200	Social Security
	16,000	Pension
	6,000	Investment Income
	$42,200	
Assets:	$100,000	Money market & CDs
	225,000	Home, Free and Clear
	25,000	Car
	$350,000	

Liabilities: 0

Net Worth: $350,000

Recommendation:

You are both very conservative and while you want to maintain your income, you don't want to risk principal. Because of the low returns you are getting on your money, you can take 65% of your cash, put it in AAA-rated corporate bond funds and maintain the same income you are getting now. You could then put 20% of your money in a balance fund which should increase your return, and 15% in an index fund. The index fund will serve as inflation protection and provide some growth to your portfolio.

Figure 18-5 Portfolio Recommendation

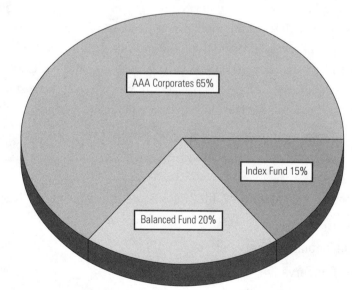

CASE STUDY NO. 6

Background:

Investors: Husband, 45 and wife, 36, they have 2 children, 1 boy of 16, 1 girl of 13

Education: Advanced degrees

Occupation: Husband is an architect, wife is an attorney

Goals: 1. Education planning for the children.

2. Retirement planning.

Risk Tolerance: Moderate to Aggressive.

Income: $145,000

Assets:	$365,000	Home
	65,000	Retirement Benefits
	15,000	Cash
	<u>20,000</u>	Personal Property
	$465,000	

Liabilities:	$275,000	Mortgage on the Home
	5,000	Credit Card Debt
	<u>60,000</u>	Automobiles
	$340,000	

Net Worth: $125,000

Recommendation:

Because education planning is a big concern I recommend that you immediately start an accumulation program to fund each of the children's education. I recommend a growth stock fund.

At the present time, each of you are funding a 401-K available through your employer. I recommended that you also start individual mutual fund IRAs. Each year you can invest an additional $2,000 in the IRAs and put them in growth or aggressive growth mutual funds. While the IRA is currently not deductible because you already have retirement plans at your work, the income would nevertheless compound tax free and would be the best method of growing dollars over the long term. By reviewing the holdings of your present 401-Ks you have acknowledged that you are allowed to change the mutual fund selection on a quarterly basis. Presently, you are holding a combination of bonds and mutual funds. Based on the current economy of slow growth with potentially declining interest rates, I recommended that you switch to growth mutual funds within your 401-K portfolio and perhaps diversify with up to 25% in international markets, which is an additional alternative that your plan allows.

College Education Accounts: 100% Growth Funds

Husband New IRA: 100% Growth Funds

Wife New IRA: 100% Growth Funds

For long-term growth I recommeded they set aside 5% of their income for the future. This would be done only after the first two recommendations were achieved and we acknowledge it might not be done until they got new raises. I recommended that they consider this a long-term savings account and to be more aggressive because any decline would have recovery time.

Figure 18-6   Portfolio Recommendation

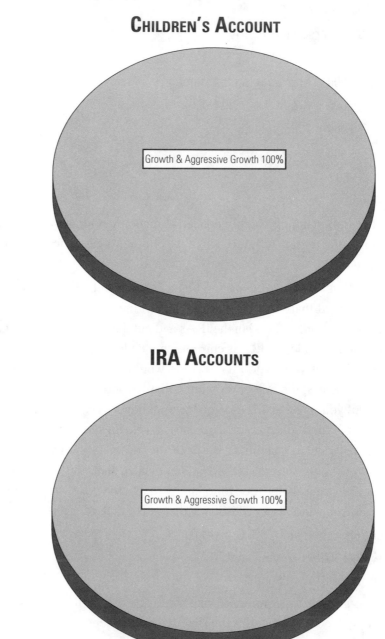

CHILDREN'S ACCOUNT

Growth & Aggressive Growth 100%

IRA ACCOUNTS

Growth & Aggressive Growth 100%

401-K

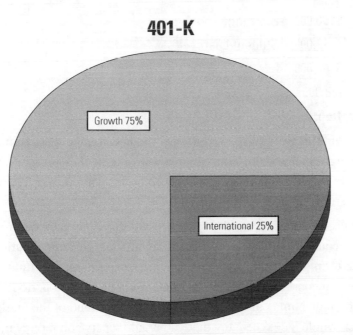

Growth 75%

International 25%

CASE STUDY NO. 7

Background:

Investor: Sue, age 38, divorced, two children, ages 10 and 8.

Education: High School

Occupation: Interior Designer

Risk Tolerance: Moderate

Goals:

Income:	$26,000	
	24,000	(Child Support)
	$50,000	
Assets:	$200,000	Cash (Divorce Settlement)
	50,000	Equity in Home
	10,000	Personal Property
	$260,000	

Liabilities: $100,000 Mortgage

2,000 Student Loan

$102,000

Net Worth: $158,000

Recommendation:

At the present time, you have no retirement plan coverage. I recommend that you set aside enough money from your savings to fund an IRA account. Your current income plus the child support are adequate to cover your current needs as well as funding the retirement plan.

Your major concern is the $200,000 lump sum that you received in your divorce settlement. Because you do not need current income, my recommendation is that you plan for long-term growth and structure the investment in mutual funds. If you ever need additional income then some of the funds could be sold off periodically to it. By using growth mutual funds in the current economy and trend of the market, I believe that the return would far exceed any that you would receive on money markets, CDs, or bonds. By structuring a sell-off on an as-needed basis, you achieve the option of generating income when necessary and at the same time strive for higher growth. Under the present economy, I suggest that you put 25% of your money into an aggressive growth fund, 25% into a growth fund, 25% into a growth & income fund, and the final 25% split equally between international funds and an index fund comprised of the S & P 500. Using this scenario of asset allocation, you would be diversified and yet maintain a heavy emphasis on long-term growth. The small portion of international funds gives the possibility of some additional profits should the international markets grow faster than the U.S. market. I advise that you establish a mutual fund account with one of the major discount brokerage firms that offered a mutual fund marketplace selection of no-load mutual funds. By utilizing no-load funds, you would not have to pay a commission on entering the funds. And if you would need to periodically sell some of the funds in order to generate income, there would be no fee or commission for those individual sales.

Figure 18-7   Portfolio Recommendation

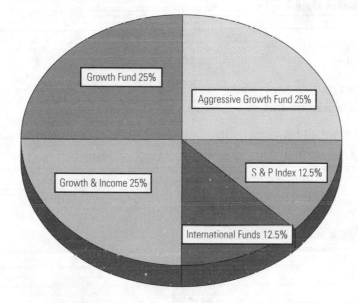

STRATEGIES FOR YOUR LIFE

Now that you have practiced reviewing other people's situations, it is a good time to review your own. Go to Chapter 3 and complete the financial profile I have included for you. If you are married, go through it with your spouse. After you have completed the form, make specific recommendations for yourself that are consistent with your long-term goals. This process will help you put into practice everything that was discussed in this book. If you would like help during this process and actually receive our input, call and set up an appointment for your own 30-minute Financial Quick Start. We'll be happy to go through your profile with you and make specific recommendations. For further information about cost and to schedule an appointment, call 1-800-333-3700.

LET'S REMEMBER THIS:

▶ Just because a strategy doesn't work for you now doesn't mean it won't be important to you as your life changes.

▶ Of all the mutual fund strategies we've talked about you only need one—the one that works for you.

▶ Your financial life is an evolving process. Don't forget to review your situation frequently and consider new investment strategies for new problems.

QUESTIONS AND ANSWERS ON MUTUAL FUNDS

▼

1. **I'm worried about a mutual fund crash. I've heard that many people had trouble selling out of the mutual funds in the 1987 crash. Is there anything I can do to protect myself?**

   A: There certainly is nothing wrong with being worried about a mutual fund crash. A good worry about anything is okay, as long as it doesn't prevent you from action. The same is true with investing in mutual funds. There is nothing wrong with a little worry as long it doesn't keep you from investing. You are correct that many people did have difficulty getting out of their mutual funds in the 1987 crash. This was the first time the mutual funds had experienced mass selling, and the funds weren't ready for such a problem. Since that time the industry has grown a lot and is better equipped to handle a situation like that. Nevertheless, there are a couple of ways to protect yourself. First, see if your mutual fund company will accept a sale order by fax. This eliminates the time delay of mail. And second, consider using a discount broker to handle all of your mutual fund trades. Charles Schwab, Fidelity Investments, and Jack White and Company all have reasonably priced mutual fund trading programs that were discussed in this book. In each case, they are also able to immediately sell your funds with a simple phone call.

2. **Are large funds better to invest in than small funds?**

   A: No. A mutual fund needs to have at least $5 to $10 million as a minimum operating base in order to handle the normal operating expenses of running the fund without devastating the overall return on investment. Frequently, in the early stages of a mutual fund, the investment advisor or management group will agree to absorb all of the expenses so its return is not weighed down by those expenses. Once the fund achieves a certain level of money under management, the mutual fund company begins to charge it with some of the operating expenses. A maximum expense number will be stated in the prospectus.

Large funds have a different problem. The difficulty of managing large funds is the constant task of continuing to find good investment vehicles in which to put all of that money. It is one thing to be responsible for investing $50 million and finding a good investment for that amount. It is quite another task to invest $400 million in great investment opportunities.

Large fund managers are also faced with another problem. Once they find a stock that is a winner, the size of your investment can actually begin to effect the price. For example, as you continue on your buying spree of a particular stock, you may soon find that your position in that one stock is so large that if you change your mind and begin to sell out of that stock, you will drive down the market price of that stock. The result, of course, is that the winning investment is less attractive simply because of your selling volume. In short, spend less time worrying about the size and more about performance.

3. **Would you invest in a newly formed mutual fund?**

A: As previously mentioned, the problem with investing in new mutual funds is that the cost and expense ratio are high compared to the return of the overall portfolio. We also mentioned that this is typically reduced by the fact that the mutual fund company itself agrees to absorb those costs. However, the most glaring reason to avoid newly formed funds is the fact that they have no track record. This can be tremendously minimized if this is a new fund formed by a successful money manager who has simply expanded his options. For example, if a manager has a long-term track record in a particular fund and now, because of the size of that fund, has decided to form a new fund with similar goals and objectives as the previous one, then the risks are minimal. These funds are frequently called clones. On the other hand, if the new fund is totally different it may be outside the money manager's expertise and should not be considered.

The bottom line to this discussion is to investigate the new fund to find out what its purpose is, who is running the fund, and what their experience is with this type of investment.

4. **Can I lose a lot of money in mutual funds?**

A: Yes. Just because a mutual fund has many advantages, such as diversity of investing, it does not mean that investors should throw caution to the wind when investing in mutual funds. There are extremely aggressive mutual funds just as there are very conservative ones. You should always be mindful of the objectives of the mutual fund and its manager, trying to discern what its track record has been and what its prospects for the future are. Prudence should always be the guide in any investing, including mutual funds.

5. **I cannot afford to lose principal. Should I avoid mutual funds?**

A: Not necessarily. Mutual funds, as mentioned throughout this book, are simply an umbrella, a vehicle if you will, to invest in particular kinds of companies or products. Just as the previous question addressed that there are potential risks with mutual funds, they can also be used to invest in conservative investments such as money markets and can provide diversification even among those conservative investments. The key question to recognize and to analyze is: What are the objectives of the mutual fund and what is the money manager investing your money in? If the underlying mutual fund investment is conservative and protects your principal, then the mutual fund will also protect your principal.

6. **I need current income, but I believe that growth funds will build my account faster. Is there a way to have my cake and eat it too?**

A: Yes, there is. Many people believe that income investing can only be done by investing in an underlying security that produces income. The thought is that unless a stock produces a dividend, it doesn't produce income. Nothing could be further from the truth and this is important to understand in structuring portfolios for people who need income. I believe that growth mutual funds are ideal to create structured portfolios that throw off income. For example, during a bull market, an investor who selects good long-term growth stocks that appreciate at a much faster rate than a bond fund can achieve substantially higher yields. This investor only needs to work with his mutual fund company to structure a systematic withdrawal program that sells off a certain percentage of his fund each month. The sale proceeds are automatically sent to the investor producing a steady income stream.

7. Why don't I just invest in last year's best performing fund and forget everything else?

A: I wish it were that simple. There are no perfect long-term investments despite everyone's desire to have one. The practical result of this statement is that last year's winning mutual fund may very well be this year's worst performing fund, and for a variety of reasons. One reason may be that interest rates were rapidly declining during the past year, but are now in a stable or even increasing mode. This one economic fact would have a tremendous difference in the selection of the best mutual fund to invest in for the upcoming year.

8. Do investors make a built-in profit on closed-end funds sold at a discount?

A: The answer is yes and no. Closed-end funds that may be sold at a discount allow investors to make that spread if the fund is successful. While this does occur, it is much more frequent that a fund that sells at a 10% discount today will likely be selling at the same 10% discount in the near future. Anyone who makes an investment simply planning to make money on the discount is making a mistake.

One successful strategy to watch for are announcements that a closed-end fund will definitely convert to an open-end fund. On the date of conversion, the fund must sell at its net asset value (NAV). Consequently, between the announced date and the conversion date, the spread will be eliminated. If you buy during this time, you will profit on the closing of the spread. However, what happens to the actual underlying security during this time will depend on the market.

Never buy a closed-end mutual fund when it is initially sold or issued. The reason is that you pay a commission of up to 10%, and from then on the fund generally trades at that discounted amount.

9. Do I need a money manager?

A: Money managers are in the business to increase an investor's overall return. If you have found over your investment life that you can experience a 10% return based upon your investment selections, and by investigating money managers you discover that a certain one can increase your yield to a 15% overall return because of his experience in the marketplace, the answer is clear that using the money manager is the best option. Money managers are simply tools to increase your yield. If they can help you, they are worth it and you should use them. If they cannot help you, nor save you time or money, then don't use them.

10. Do load funds perform better than no-load funds?

A: There have been many studies based on the comparison between a load fund (commissioned) and a no-load fund. While the commissioned salesmen would like for you to believe that their funds are better, that simply has not been born out by the statistics. On the other hand, that does not mean that simply because a fund has a load to it that it should be excluded. There have historically been load funds that have produced exceptionally well. The analogy I would make is very similar to the one I used in answering the question about expenses: You should always be more concerned about your net return and less about expenses and commissions. Both of these costs are simply one element in the total review of a particular fund.

As a general rule, I would recommend that you invest in no-load mutual funds as opposed to loaded ones. If, in isolated cases, you can determine that the return of a particular fund is exceptional, then that fund should not be excluded just because a commission is charged.

11. How much do I need to get started investing in mutual funds?

A: All mutual funds have investment minimums. As a general rule, they require from $500 to $1,000 on an initial investment and allow periodic investments of $50 thereafter. The important thing to remember is to simply get started. How many times have you seen those magnificent charts that show that a small investment today will be worth millions of dollars in the future? The funny thing about it is that these charts are true if you will get started and if you will keep compounding your return.

12. If mutual funds provide diversification, does that mean that they will simply produce average returns?

A: No. The negative aspect of diversification can be similar to averaging where you throw out the best and the worst and wind up with the middle. This is minimized in most mutual funds because of the objectives set by the fund. In general, the mutual fund is designed to accomplish a specific purpose and uses a selection of stocks to accomplish that goal. Had you been able to select the absolute best stock within that portfolio, you would have done better than the fund, but the skill of the fund managers tends to keep the returns higher than simply the average.

13. Is the concept of mutual funds a good investment concept?

A: Mutual funds have been around for a long time. In fact, I think the first fund was started in the mid-1920s. For quite a few years, they languished without capturing the attention of the investment community until the mid-1970s when mutual funds got their first scandal during the Burnie Cornfield era when a great deal of money was actually stolen from the accounts of investors. Things have changed since that time, including much closer regulation by the SEC. Today, there are literally thousands of mutual funds. In fact there are more mutual funds than there are individual stocks on the New York Stock Exchange. Today, the total amount of money invested is more than $2,000,000,000,000. While that is no assurance that mutual funds are a good investment, it is a comfort to know that they have been studied and examined by some of the brightest people in the investment world and they have collectively determined that they are good investments for most people.

14. Are there a lot of differences between bond funds?

A: There is probably as much difference in bond funds as there is in individual stock funds, although they are frequently lumped together. The primary difference that exists is in the length of time until maturity. This is particularly important because the longer maturing bonds are subject to interest rate fluctuations and can cause principal loss if you are on the wrong side of the interest rate fluctuation. For the investor who is unaware of these differences, it can be a rude awakening to find that what they thought was a conservative bond investment has in reality turned out to be a very aggressive investment that has lost principal.

Short-term bond funds tend to have a lifetime duration between one and five years. These funds can be made up of corporate, treasury, or even municipal short-term bond funds. Intermediate-term bond funds are made up of funds with durations from five to fifteen years. These funds can also be made up of treasuries, corporates, junk bonds, or tax-free municipals. The third category, long-term bond funds, are generally funds from fifteen to thirty years. These bond funds are also broken down into the four categories just listed.

15. **Are all stock funds growth-oriented?**

A: No. Stock funds can be income-oriented, growth-oriented, aggressive growth-oriented, or a combination thereof. The underlying factor depends on the type of stock the funds invest in. Some funds invest in stocks seeking to get high dividends. These funds are pleased when they can also achieve capital gains, but their major intention was to receive income from the dividends. These funds will invest in securities, either preferred stocks or convertible bonds, looking primarily for the generation of income.

16. **What do you think about social responsibility funds?**

A: Social responsibility funds are relatively new to the marketplace and are part of the new trend to create a different fund geared toward whatever the buying population wants. My personal opinion is that if you believe in a "cause" or a concept, put your money into a good growth fund and take the profits produced from that fund and invest it separately in the "cause" or concept. From an investment philosophy, I don't believe that "causes" have a place in investment.

17. **The price of my fund dropped in value according to the listing in the newspaper, but my advisor tells me I haven't lost any money. How can this be?**

A: The problem with watching the price of a fund strictly in the newspaper is that you don't know about the distributions the funds are making. When a fund makes a distribution directly to the shareholders, you get more shares of the fund, but when this occurs, it reduces the share price of the fund by the exact amount of the distribution. Consequently, even though you would have had a distribution sent to you, it would appear that the price of your fund has lost value. It hasn't, however, because you've gotten more shares. The best way to figure exactly how much you've made or lost on your investment is to compare the total value of your holdings to the total amount of your original investment. This simply means taking the total number of shares and multiplying it by the current price of the fund to determine your total current value. Compare that amount to the amount you invested and you will find out how much your increase or decrease has been.

18. **I'm not very good at math; is there an easy way for me to find out my return on my mutual fund investment?**

    A: Yes, there is. Every mutual fund has a toll-free 800 number that has a customer representative waiting on the other end of the line. They will be happy to calculate your return for you because that is what keeps them in business. You pay for their salary so don't be afraid to take advantage of the service.

19. **I've been reading that mutual fund newsletters are a waste of time and money. What do you think?**

    A: Well, remember, I'm biased because I write a mutual fund newsletter. However, let me hasten to point out that the real answer is that it depends upon what you personally get out of a newsletter. Let me suggest that you run a little test for yourself. Take one-half of your portfolio and invest it totally on your own. Take the other half of your portfolio and invest following your favorite newsletter. If you can do better than your mutual fund newsletter advisor, I'd cancel the newsletter. If the newsletter makes you more money than it cost, I'd renew the subscription. By the way, your test shouldn't really cost anything because most newsletters will give you a money-back trial subscription for a short period of time so that if it doesn't work out, you can cancel and ask for your money back.

20. **There is a lot of computer software on the market today designed for helping mutual fund investors. Is it worth my money and time?**

    A: Although I am not in the computer software business, my answer is similar to the response regarding newsletters. If the software can help you increase your return, then it is worthwhile. In our business, which is managing client investments, we spend thousands of dollars each year buying new software and maintaining old software in order to create an edge on the marketplace. Fortunately, there are some products available for individual investors that I think do almost as well, and certainly wouldn't help give you an additional edge that you wouldn't have without software. Some suggestions on places to contact include Valueline (1-800-833-0046) and Morningstar (1-312-696-6000).

21. **I'm very concerned about investing in anything that is not FDIC or FSLIC insured. Should that concern carry over into mutual funds?**

A: Yes, it should. Mutual funds are not government insured unless the underlying stock or asset that they have purchased is government insured. Consequently, if that is an absolute feature of your investment criteria, you should only consider funds backed by the U.S. Treasury, securities, or other U.S. Government agency issues. Remember, there is always a risk/reward ratio to investing; if you are not willing to accept the higher risk, your reward will likely be lower.

22. **I've been investing many years and believe I'd do better investing in individual stocks. Can you give me one good reason why I should invest in mutual funds?**

    A: In the opening chapter of this book I give you eight good reasons why you should invest in mutual funds. Nevertheless, that might not be enough. In the end, it is really a personal issue based on both your ability and desire to analyze stocks. The best way to determine this for yourself is to give it a test. Take a portion of your readily available dollars for investment, put half of it in individual stocks and half of it in mutual funds. Run the test for a period of a couple of years and make a determination: Which of those portfolios has produced the highest return? If you consistently can outperform a mutual fund by investing in stocks, I have a simple answer for you: Invest in stocks.

23. **We have just had a new grandchild and are thinking about setting aside money for a college education. Would you consider mutual funds?**

    A: I think mutual funds would make an excellent choice for setting aside money for a college education. You might want to also consider some of the funds that have specific programs for trusts for minor children. One contact source would be the 20th Century Gift Trusts, telephone 1-800-345-2021. Two other good options are either Fidelity, (1-800-544-8888) or Vanguard, (1-800-662-7447).

24. **I've been in the real estate business all of my life and have been successful at buying and selling property. Why should I invest in mutual funds?**

    A: Diversification. If you are experienced in real estate, then you know one thing to be certain: There are numerous booms and busts. While I would encourage you to continue to invest in what you're good at, don't forget there are other options, and diversification is a protection against catastrophe.

25. **I've heard people using the term "contrarian investing." What does that mean? Are there funds that adopt that philosophy?**

A: Contrarian investing simply means that you are going against the current or conventional wisdom in investing. As I've mentioned throughout this book, there are mutual funds designed around every form of investing and contrarian investing certainly has its own funds. Two that I am most familiar with are the Fidelity Contra Fund and Vanguard Windsor. These funds both tend to buy securities that they believe are presently undervalued because of current overly-pessimistic views in the marketplace.

26. **What do you think of gold and other precious metal funds?**

A: My wife thinks that gold is wonderful to wear. I agree it looks nice on her, but it makes for a lousy investment. Gold and precious metals have traditionally been extremely speculative investments and lots of people have lost money because of the lure of potential incredible profits. Someday big profits may again be made by investing in gold and precious metals. In the meantime, however, I'd suggest you make a lot of money in growth and aggressive-growth stocks and buy gold for you or your spouse to wear.

Your Questions Answered

One of the purposes of this book was to answer your questions about mutual fund investing. We hope we have done that. However, if you have additional questions that you can't seem to get answered, drop us a note and we'll try to help. Please enclose a self-addressed, stamped envelope for our reply. We won't promise to answer every question, but we'll do our best.

> The Mutual Fund Advisor
> 520 Crown Oak Centre Drive
> Longwood, FL 32750

Money Talks Summary

▼

1. Mutual fund distributions can be made up of the following:

   ▶ Dividends, which are earnings paid out by the companies in a mutual fund portfolio;

   ▶ Interest payments from bond or money market holdings;

   ▶ And capital gains representing profits on stocks held in the mutual fund. These are long-term gains if held at least twelve months and short term gains if held less.

2. Dollar Cost Averaging is a system of making periodic purchases of an investment. By buying at all price levels, your costs will be averaged.

3. Risk is a word that means different things to different people. Therefore, if anyone ever asks you about your risk tolerance, you need to find out what they mean. For example, while most people think of risk as "market risk" (loss due to price fluctuations), there is also inflation risk, tax risk, volatility risk, and time value risk.

4. Telephone switching is a method of moving your investment from one fund in the fund family to another by a simple phone call. The advantage of this service is that you can move quickly from one fund to another as changes in the market or the specific fund dictate.

5. 12-B-1 fees are built-in marketing fees that some funds charge investors. These fees are used to pay brokerage firms and other investment advisors who sold you the fund. The fees are like hidden commissions because they allow the fund to say it is "no load," but they use these fees to pay the broker. Redemption fees are rear loads on commissions charged when you sell a fund. These fees are used by mutual funds to discourage investors from moving out of their fund family.

6. Cash management account is the generic term for the service that provides a master account linking all of your financial activities together. The mutual

fund families all have their own name for the account. An example of one such service is the Fidelity Ultra Account sponsored by Fidelity Investments. The account will show your monthly activity for checking, debit card, money market accounts, mutual funds, and stock purchases.

7. The term "value" as used with value funds can be misleading. Most fund managers think of a stock held in a value fund as having value because its price has underperformed compared to the intrinsic worth of the stock. Consequently, the stocks in a value fund may be unknown. This definition is frequently different from many investors who would think of a value stock as being fully valued like some blue chip stocks.

8. Dollar-cost averaging promotes continuous investing in the same stock at all price levels. Systematic investing promotes continuous investing, but uses different securities based on current market trends.

9. Market timing is a strategy of always trying to be invested "in" the market during up trends and "out" of the market during down trends.

10. A price range chart is a graph that shows a line made from connecting daily points representing the price of a security. When the dots are connected the line that is produced is called the price line.

11. Fundamental analysis of a company involves focusing on the performance of a company's sales earnings and profits, their relationship to each other, and their relationship to the price of the stock in the company.

12. Technical analysis is the study of the price patterns of a company's stock and its relationship to the market.

13. Relative Strength Momentum (RSM) is a comparison between a specific fund, the general market, and all other funds of its type. The higher its RSM, the faster its price is moving compared to the others.

14. "Selling short" means selling mutual funds you don't own but have temporarily borrowed from a brokerage firm. You gain a profit if you can replace them by buying shares in the same fund at a lower price.

15. A fixed annuity provides a guaranteed minimum by an insurance company. A variable annuity is invested in mutual funds and its return is dependent on the success of the mutual fund.

Dollars & Sense Summary

▼

1. Use "Mutual Fund Families" to quickly and easily "switch" from one mutual fund to another as the economy or performance of the fund dictates. For example, you are presently invested in a long-term bond fund with an average duration of 25 years. You notice that interest rates are increasing and because that change will make the bonds of your fund less valuable, you call the fund and switch from their bond fund to their money market fund. The money market fund will pay higher dividends as interest rates rise.

2. Use mutual funds to diversify portfolio risk normally associated with individual stock and at a fraction of the cost, both in terms of portfolio size requirements and transaction cost.

3. Automatically reinvest your mutual fund dividends to take advantage of dollar-cost averaging and the growth affects of compounding your returns.

4. Use money market accounts as a temporary place to park your money between investments in equity or bond funds.

5. Use growth funds to build assets for the long term.

6. Use aggressive growth funds in strong markets, but watch them carefully for price volatility.

7. Use funds with a blend of high-rated and lower-rated bond funds to diversify both income and risk.

8. Use growth/income funds to balance your portfolio between income-producing investments and those that offer growth and inflation protection.

9. Use sector funds to take advantage of specialized knowledge in an industry.

10. Use global and overseas funds to take advantage of world economics.

11. **THE NO-LOAD EXAMPLE:** A novice invests or buys in a new mutual fund from his local bank that has a 6% load fund. During the first year, it has a great year and returns 20%. Unfortunately, the net yield drops back to 14%

because of the load. Not a bad yield, but the load was certainly a lot to make up. If the investor has to switch funds in order to maintain the yield and he doubles up on the commission, 6% on the first fund and 6% on the second fund, then the yield for the year now drops to 8%. Add a 2% management fee the fund charges and you net only 6%. You can now see why you're not making any money.

If instead of using loaded funds, you had used no-load funds and switched funds within a fund family that doesn't charge a commission, your yield would have been 20% less a 1% management fee for a 19% effective yield. The result of this brief exercise will show you quickly why no-load funds have proliferated throughout the marketplace and why loads and management fees are important to your overall return.

12. Use no-load funds to lower your cost of investing.

13. Never buy a closed-end fund at its initial offering because you will immediately lose value based on the cost of the offering.

14. Set honest and realistic financial goals and readjust them periodically as your life needs change. To cement the goals in your mind, write them down and commit to them.

15. Before you invest:

   ▶ Pay off all high-interest rate credit cards.

   ▶ Participate in any matching funds savings programs available through your corporation.

   ▶ Start a retirement program: IRA, Keough, SEP, 401-K, or 403-B.

16. Request several prospectuses from mutual fund companies and compare them to the points discussed in this chapter.

17. Funds' portfolios change frequently. Consequently, before you invest, feel free to contact the fund directly to see the current makeup of its portfolio.

18. One service that you may want to inquire about early on is tax service. Some funds and discount brokerage companies will do all of your capital gains and loss calculations for you. This is a big time-saver and reduces your accounting bill.

19. When you set up the mutual fund account, find out the specific feature for redemption. Many funds require written instructions and that your signature be signed under a bank guarantee. That means you must physically sign the fund's redemption request before a bank officer. This is different than a notary public. This process can take several days so I recommend making up a liquidation request form ahead of time, get your signature guaranteed, and keep the form on file until you need to use it. Date it only when you use it.

20. To avoid delays in selling your funds, don't take actual possession of your securities. Not only does this save time when you sell the fund, it avoids the expense you incur (1%–2%) if you lose your certificates.

21. When comparing returns on various mutual funds, make sure the comparisons are made using the same calculation methods and include all distributions.

22. Great mutual fund managers are like star athletes. There are only a few of them and they are paid well. Getting to know who the best managers are is just as important as knowing the holdings of a fund.

23. Investing only in each year's top-ranked fund has not proven to be a successful strategy. The reason? Changing conditions. Managers change, the markets change, the economy changes. Any one of these factors can affect future returns.

24. Use cash management accounts like a jumbo savings account, running all of your credit card, checking, and mutual fund purchases through the same account. This will simplify your year-end tax accounting tremendously.

25. Five steps before you buy stock mutual funds:
    ▶ Know your goals;
    ▶ Know your needs;
    ▶ Know your risk tolerance;
    ▶ Research and analyze the funds; and
    ▶ Monitor your selections.

26. The three critical steps to selecting a mutual fund investment include:
    ▶ Historical performance;
    ▶ Internal makeup of the fund selected; and

▶ The current trend of the market in general and the specific fund under analysis.

27. While past performance is never a guarantee of future success, it does tell you a lot about what the fund has done in various market environments and provides information to help you understand what it might do in the present environment.

28. Use clone funds to take advantage of successful funds that are now closed to new buyers. Make sure the manager is the same and that the objectives are also still the same. This information can be found in the prospectus or by calling the service representative.

29. Contrary to the media hype, derivatives are not all bad. The recent problem with derivatives was that investors didn't understand what it was or more particularly, what it was derived from. Consequently, some investors were putting their money in more volatile securities than they thought. If you understand the derivative and what it is, you may consciously find that they have a place in your portfolio. As always, the key is understanding.

30. Five key features for bond fund selection:

   ▶ Cost, including on-going expenses;

   ▶ Management expertise;

   ▶ Age of fund;

   ▶ Type compared to your needs; and

   ▶ Quality.

31. Rebalance your investment portfolio every year or two to make sure you are still maintaining the investment allocation percentage you wanted to accomplish when you set up the plan.

32. The broader the index, the more diverse your investment and the less it is subject to volatility.

33. Index funds allow passive investors to participate in the overall trend of the international market and reduce some risk of individual funds.

34. Use the direction of the economy to decide whether to be in stocks, bonds, or money markets.

35. When interest rates fall, the stock market rises. This is when investors should have their funds in equity stocks or bonds.

36. Rising inflation and rising interest rates will foretell a bad stock market ahead.

37. Use real interest rates as the best predictor of the future of the market.

38. An increasing Produce Price Index (PPI) is bad for the stock market and a decreasing PPI predicts a good market ahead.

39. Low unemployment (high employment) predicts an increase in inflation and lower stock prices ahead.

40. Use moving averages to help you quickly determine the direction of a stock, bond, mutual fund, or entire market. For stocks, a good short-term moving average is 15 weeks and a good long-term moving average is 39 weeks.

41. The Profitline Strategy uses a long-term, 39-week moving average to provide stability and safety. In addition, we use a more aggressive, 15-week moving average to provide an early warning system.

42. Use Relative Strength Momentum (RSM) to quickly compare funds to see which ones are doing better than the overall market.

43. Use moving average comparisons and broad market indices to give a strong indication of the current market direction.

44. Use sector funds to take advantage of specialized information you may have about an industry. A computer consultant may learn how to make more money on his investments by investing in the computers, software, and technology sector.

45. Because sector funds cover every major industry, one will be performing well no matter what the economy. Use sectors to take advantage of your knowledge of economic shifts.

46. To select the best performing funds use the information available from both technical and fundamental indicators.

47. The two best ways to set up an account for sector fund investing is through either a discount broker or directly with a large fund family that has a wide range of mutual fund selections.

48. Margin interest is deductible as interest used for investments. This advantage lowers your real cost of the transaction by the amount of your marginal tax bracket.

49. Use international funds to add an additional type of diversification to your investment portfolio and to provide alternatives when the U.S. markets are down.

50. Emerging nations offer unusual opportunities not available in developed countries. While the growth opportunities are big, remember that additional rewards are always associated with added risk.

51. Three added risks of international investing are:
    ▶ Currency risk;
    ▶ Lower government control over international public companies; and
    ▶ Economic and political changes are less stable than in the U.S.

52. International stock mutual funds come in three basic types:
    ▶ Those which are diversified over a wide area (United States and a minimum of three major foreign markets);
    ▶ Those which diversify over a particular region (European, Pacific Rim); and
    ▶ Those which allow the investor to target one specific foreign market. The last type is more commonly known as a *single-country fund* (Mexico fund, Korea fund).

53. Trading can be done in a retirement plan without regard to tax considerations because all tax on earnings within a plan is deferred until money is taken out of the plan.

54. Even if you no longer qualify for a deductible IRA, you should continue to make your contributions because all income grows tax-deferred.

55. If your company offers a matching contribution plan where they contribute a certain dollar amount equal to your own savings, make sure you maximize this plan before you do any other investing. Matching dollar plans gives you a built-in return that you can't get anywhere else.

56. Take an active role in your 401-K or 403-B plan. Encourage your plan administrator to establish flexible alternatives to provide the best investment solutions.

57. Mutual funds are taxed on three different sources of income: dividends, the fund's capital gain distribution to you, and your capital gains generated on profitable sales of the funds you own.

58. Depending on your marginal tax bracket, an investor may do better from an after-tax return to buy tax-free municipals instead of taxable bonds. Always make your final analysis based on "after-tax yields" instead of "pre-tax" yields.

59. Use variable annuities as a way to combine mutual fund investing on a tax-deferred basis.

60. Use independent rating services to help you determine the safety of any annuity you review.

61. **PLANNING STRATEGIES:** Because the 10% penalty is levied on withdrawals before the age of $59^1/_2$, many investors past that age also use annuities for short-term goals. New products are structured more like CDs and do not have the longer withdrawal penalties previously mentioned. These investments, frequently called CD Annuities, allow you to get yields slightly higher than CDs but are tax-deferred until you use the money.

62. Because you don't pay capital gains on annuities you need not concern yourself with the tax consequences of trading or switching between your investments held in the annuity.

63. Use annuities as an additional private retirement program. Your initial contribution is not tax deferred, but the money you make on it in the annuity grows tax deferred.

RESOURCES

▼

In this section, I have listed resources that I believe will be helpful to you. I have reviewed or personally subscribed to the materials provided here.

American Association of Individual Investors
612 North Michigan Avenue
Chicago, IL 60611

This is a non-profit organization that not only sells books and tapes on investing, but also has small investor groups throughout the country that you can join. There is a $48 per year membership fee.

Baron's
200 Burnett Road
Chicopee, MA 01020

This is an excellent weekly publication that gives an overview of the market.

Dow Jones-Irwin Guide to Investment Software
by Robert Schwabach

For information about this book, contact Dow Jones-Irwin or your local bookstore. This is an excellent book that explains the use of financial software.

Stock Market Logic
by Norman Fosbach

This book is available through the *Mutual Fund Forecaster,* 3471 North Federal Highway, Ft. Lauderdale, FL 33306, telephone: 800-327-6720. This is an excellent overall book about the stock market and investing. It is frequently given free to subscribers of the *Mutual Fund Forecaster.*

Technical Analysis Explained
by Martin J. Pring, McGraw Hill, 1995

This is a very technical, highbrow explanation of technical analysis. It is for people who are serious about using the technical analysis approach.

Fund Exchange
1200 West Lake Avenue North, Suite 507
Seattle, WA 98101-3530
206-285-8877

This newsletter is written by Paul Merriman who is a market timer. The cost of the service is $99 per year and includes a telephone hotline.

Hulbert Financial Digest
316 Commerce Street
Alexandria, VA 32314
703-683-5905

This publication is written by Mark Hulbert. He is also a columnist for *Forbes* magazine. Each year, Mr. Hulbert analyzes all newsletter writers and keeps a running tally of their historical performance.

Mutual Fund Forecaster
3471 North Federal Highway
Ft. Lauderdale, FL 33306
800-327-6720

This is one of the publications issued by the Norman Fosbach organization. Ask for a complete list of their offerings.

Mutual Fund Advisor
520 Crown Oak Centre Drive
Longwood, FL 32750
800-333-3700

This publication is written by the author of this book, J.W. Dicks. Because I am biased, I won't tell you how good the publication is; just call and ask for a free copy.

Mutual Fund Investing
7811 Montrose Road
Potomac, MD 20854
301-340-2100

This newsletter is written by Jay Schabacker. The cost is $99 per year and it has a telephone hotline.

No-Load Fund X
235 Montgomery Street
San Francisco, CA 94104
415-986-7979

This newsletter is written by Burton Barry. Mr. Barry follows an upgrading system urging his investors to upgrade their mutual funds periodically based on performances indicated in his newsletter.

No-Load Investor
P.O. Box 283
Hastings-on-Hudson, NY 10706
914-693-7420

This newsletter is written by Sheldon Jacobs who also published a book about investing in mutual funds. Cost of the subscription is $82 per year.

Peter Daigg Investment Letter
65 Lakefront Drive
Akron, OH 44319
330-644-2782

This newsletter is written by Peter Daigg and has a market approach to investing. The cost is $250 per year.

Telephone Switch Newsletter
P.O. Box 2538
Huntington Beach, CA 92647
714-898-2588

This publication was originally started by Dick Fabian but has now been turned over to his son, Doug, who also is doing an excellent job. The publication follows the moving average system.

Investor's Business Daily
12655 Beatrice Street
Los Angeles, CA 90066
800-831-2525

This is a daily newspaper. It is an excellent publication written for the serious investor and includes special charts and graphs similar to those explained in this book.

The Wall Street Journal
200 Burnett Road
Chicopee, MA 01020
800-221-1940

This is the grand-daddy of investment publications and requires no comment.

Morningstar, Inc.
53 West Jackson Boulevard
Chicago, IL 60604
800-876-5005

This organization provides extensive mutual fund coverage with a variety of services ranging from the expensive to a typical newsletter for investors. For further information, contact them directly.

The Valueline Mutual Fund Survey
711 3rd Avenue
New York, NY 10017-4064
800-284-7607

This organization also provides an extensive service for serious investors.

Delta Advisory Services
520 Crown Oak Centre Drive
Longwood, FL 32750
800-333-3700

This organization was founded by my long-time business partner, Charles C. Smith. The firm manages money for individual investors and retirement accounts. As a point of disclosure, I do serve as an investment advisor to the company and receive compensation for my services.

Phillips Publishing International
7811 Montrose Road
Potomac, MD 20854
800-777-5005

Phillips Publishing is one of the leading publishers of financial newsletters in the United States. Contact them and ask for a list of the newsletters that they currently publish.

Pino & Dicks
520 Crown Oak Centre Drive
Longwood, FL 32750
800-593-4257

> This is a law firm of which I am a principal. The firm specializes in representing investors throughout the country in the recovery of investment losses due to fraud or misrepresentation. For further information, or questions you may have about investment loss you have experienced, contact the firm at the number above.

Charles Schwab
101 Montgomery Street
San Francisco, CA 94104
800-526-8600

> This is a discount brokerage firm that operates the Mutual Fund One Source. This program allows investors to invest in no-load mutual funds and has a wide selection to choose from.

Jack White & Co.
9191 Town Center, 2nd Floor
San Diego, CA 92122
800-323-3263

> One of the leading discount brokerage firms that specializes in mutual fund investments and operates a no-load fund exchange system.

Fidelity Discount Brokerage
82 Devonshire Street
Boston, MA 02109
800-544-8666

> This firm operates a system of no-load mutual fund investing.

J.W. Dicks' 30-minute Financial Quick Start
520 Crown Oak Centre Drive
Longwood, FL 32750
800-333-3700

> This is a personal 30-minute counseling session I conduct to help clients quickstart their financial life. Call for information or to set an appointment.

GLOSSARY

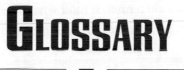

12-B-1 Fees: These are marketing fees charged by a mutual fund to promote the fund to the investing public. These fees will increase the annual cost of the fund to investors.

Aggressive Growth Funds: These have capital gains as their primary objective, but are considered more volatile than growth funds. Frequently, they will use more speculative investing techniques including leveraging funds, using options, and exercising hedging techniques in order to maximize the gains.

Annuity: An insurance product that offers a tax-deferred method of investing combined with term life insurance. There are two types: fixed and variable.

Asset Allocation: An investment theory that promotes dividing your investment into several investment baskets, each with a separate objective. It is considered a method of reducing risk.

Back-End Load: A commission paid to the mutual fund when withdrawing money from a fund.

Balanced Fund: This fund is a type of growth and income fund, but it specifically describes to investors the percentage of assets that it places in common stocks and the percentage placed in bonds. Its objective is to produce both income and growth for its investors.

Beta: A mutual fund's beta ratio indicates the fund's past volatility relative to a certain market index. The closer that the beta ranking is to 1.00, the closer its volatility is to the average of the market it is indexing. The higher the beta ranking, the more volatile the fund.

Bond Funds: These mutual funds invest in debt securities of corporations, governments, or other municipalities. They can be taxable or tax-free, depending on the type of bond.

Capital Gain: A profit made on a mutual fund when it is held for at least a one-year period. This type of gain receives a preferential lower tax treatment than the tax on ordinary income.

Cash Management Accounts: A service provided by a mutual fund acting as a master account linking all of your financial services from that fund together. The account will show your monthly activity for checking, debit cards, money market accounts, mutual funds, and stock purchases.

Certificate of Deposit (CD): Debt instruments issued by banks and savings and loan associations.

Clone Funds: A mutual fund formed by an investment company that believes a certain fund in its group has grown too large to accomplish its original plan. The new fund that is formed is identical to the successful one.

Closed-End Fund: This fund is structured opposite the open-end fund. Closed-end funds issue a set number of securities in an offering just like a new company selling stock. The price of closed-end funds fluctuates depending on the perception of the fund's performance in the marketplace.

Constant Dollar Plan: This type of investment strategy promotes maintaining a constant dollar amount in a particular type of security. This security increases in value; the amount of increase is taken out of the fund and put in a money market savings. If the amount of money in your fund decreases after a year, then you will add back to that amount the original constant dollar.

Convertibles: This type of security is a mix between a bond and stock. An investor purchases a debt instrument that pays a stated interest but is allowed to "convert" that instrument to common stock if desired.

Cost Basis: The original price of the asset you are purchasing. This is used in determining gain or loss on the sale of the asset.

Derivatives: Investments in securities that have been created from other types of securities. For example, an option to purchase a stock is a derivative of that stock.

Discount Brokerage Firms: A firm that charges lower commission in the industry, but does not normally provide as much personalized assistance as full-service brokerage firms.

Diversification: The classic investment rule that has always been illustrated by the phrase, "Don't put all of your eggs in one basket." It is the central advantage to investing in mutual funds as opposed to individual stocks.

Dividends: Payments made directly to shareholders out of the profits of a company.

Dollar-cost Averaging: A system of making periodic purchases of an investment. By buying at all price levels, your costs of the investment will be averaged to a lower price.

Equity Income Funds: These funds attempt to secure steady income for investors through the purchase of common stock for dividends and preferred stock for income.

First-In, First-Out (FIFO): The tax formulas for calculating the tax impact of mutual fund profits and losses which assume that the shares being sold are the oldest shares owned by the investor.

Fixed Annuity: An insurance product that combines term insurance with a fixed minimum return on the investment portion of the annuity.

Full Service Stock Brokerage Firm: A brokerage firm that charges the highest commission because it provides more personalized service to investors.

Fund Class: Mutual funds are frequently divided into various classes designating the type of charges that are made to individual investors. Because of the cost associated with a certain class, an investor may receive a higher return in a different class of the same mutual fund.

Fundamental Analysis: The study of a mutual fund or any security based on its internal performance, including profits and losses.

Government Security: These securities represent debts of the United States Government. Treasury securities are made up of treasury bills, notes, and bonds. One advantage of government securities is that they are backed by the full faith and credit of the United States Government.

Growth/Income Funds: These mutual funds have as their objective both current income through dividends and investment accumulation, and growth through capital appreciation.

Growth Funds: Mutual funds that have capital gains as their primary objective over current income.

Income Funds: This type of mutual fund is geared toward producing the highest income for an investor through either dividends or interest earned on the money.

Index Funds: This type of fund does not invest in individual stocks or bonds, but instead invests in a particular index made up of stocks or bonds. The advantage to this type of fund is the diversity it provides over individual stock selections.

International Funds: These funds invest in overseas companies. The funds have varying objectives similar to domestic funds and are sub-categorized into income or growth funds.

Investment Advisors: Individuals who are licensed in the securities business to give individual advice on how to manage an investor's money.

Investment Company: This is another name for mutual fund companies.

Junk Bond Fund: A mutual fund made up of lower-rated bonds.

Load Funds: Any fund that has a commission attached to it. The commissions may be front-end loaded or rear loaded.

Margin Investing: Buying a mutual fund or other security based on borrowing dollars from a brokerage firm.

Market Timing: A system of moving in and out of the stock market based on a particular set of indicators. The idea is to be invested in the market when you can produce the highest return and be out of the market when it is in a down trend.

Money Market: A type of mutual fund that invests in short-term instruments producing stabilized income. This fund has low risk with modest returns.

Moving Averages: A mathematical calculation of the price of a fund averaged out over a period of weeks. The price average is typically converted to a graph that is used to analyze the performance of the subject security. The two most popular averages are the 15-week moving average which serves as an early warning system for security holders and the longer term, 39-week moving average which serves as a sell point for investors.

Municipal Bonds: A type of bond which pays interest that is tax-free on the federal level and tax-free to the residents of the state in which the bond is issued. Because of the tax savings, they generally pay a lower yield.

Mutual Fund Family: A number of individual mutual funds offered by the same investment company under one umbrella.

Net Asset Value (NAV): The actual value of an individual share compared to the total value of all holdings of the company divided by the number of shares outstanding.

No-Load Funds: Mutual funds offered without a commission.

Open-End Fund: This is the predominant fund offered. The public is sold new shares continuously and the fund is always considered to be in the distribution phase.

Profitline Strategy: A system of investing in securities, such as mutual funds, based on an analysis between the current relationship of the price of the mutual fund and its moving averages. Additional factors, such as the fund's current relative strength, assist in the final selection of a security.

Prospectus: The legally required disclosure document for a particular type of security, such as a mutual fund.

R-Squared: This term explains the relationship between the mutual fund's individual return and a particular market index, such as the S & P 500. The higher the percentile of R-Squared, the higher the percentage that the fund's performance is due to the overall market performance and not to the individual fund.

Relative Strength Momentum (RSM): A comparison between a particular mutual fund, the performance of the general market, and all other funds of its type. The higher the RSM, the faster the price of the subject fund is moving compared to other funds.

Risk: Risk affects the return to mutual fund investors. There are many different types of risk in investing, including price fluctuation, inflation risks, tax risks, volatility risks, and time value risk.

Sector Funds: These mutual funds invest in only one specific industry or area of business, such as banking, insurance, utilities, gold, energy, etc.

Shorting Mutual Funds: A method of selling mutual funds that you don't own but have temporarily borrowed from a brokerage firm. The purpose is to attempt to buy the same fund in the open marketplace at a lower price and substitute it for the ones you borrowed, creating a profit.

Technical Analysis: The process of using technical indicators and price charts to determine the performance and direction of a particular security, such as a mutual fund.

Telephone Switching: A method of moving your investment from one fund in the fund family to another by a simple telephone call.

Value Funds: Mutual funds that concentrate on strong fundamentals in underlying stocks seeking those that are currently selling below their fundamental value based on certain financial standards.

Variable Annuity: An insurance product combined with mutual fund investing to allow investors to buy mutual funds on a tax-deferred basis. It is a way of establishing a private retirement account without being subject to the restrictions on the amount of dollars invested.

INDEX

▼

T

U

V

NOTES

NOTES

NOTES

NOTES